The NEW Totally Awesome
BUSINESS
BOOK

for Kids (and Their Parents)

Also by Arthur Bochner & Rose Bochner

*The New Totally Awesome Money Book for Kids
(and Their Parents)*

By Adriane G. Berg

Moneythink

How Not to Go Broke at 102: Achieving Everlasting Wealth

Your Wealthbuilding Years

Financial Planning for Couples

Your Kids, Your Money

Gifting to People You Love

Investment Spy (CD-ROM)

Warning: Dying May Be Hazardous to Your Wealth

How to Stop Fighting about Money and Make Some

How Good Guys Grow Rich (with Milton Gralla)

Keys to Avoiding Probate and Reducing Estate Taxes

Making Up for Lost Time

The New Totally Awesome

BUSINESS BOOK

for Kids (and Their Parents)

with Twenty Super Businesses You Can Start Right Now!

Arthur Bochner & Rose Bochner

Foreword by Adriane G. Berg

Revised and Updated Third Edition

Newmarket Press

New York

This book is published simultaneously in the United States of America and in Canada.

10 9 8 7 6 5 4 3 2 1

Library of Congress Cataloging-in-Publication Data

Bochner, Arthur Berg.
The new totally awesome business book for kids : with twenty super businesses you can start right now! / Arthur Bochner and Rose Bochner.—
Rev. and updated 3rd ed.
p. cm.
Rev. ed. of: The totally awesome business book for kids / Adriane G. Berg and Arthur Berg Bochner. 2nd ed. 2002.
Includes bibliographical references and index.
ISBN 978-1-55704-757-1 (alk. paper)

1. Small business—Management—Juvenile literature. 2. New business enterprises—Management—Juvenile literature. 3. Money-making projects for children—Juvenile literature. I. Bochner, Rose. II. Berg, Adriane G. (Adriane Gilda), 1948- Totally awesome business book for kids. III. Title.
HD62.7.B64 2007
658'.041—dc22
2007002637

Quantity Purchases
Companies, professional groups, clubs, and other organizations may qualify for special terms when ordering quantities of this title. For information contact Special Sales Department, Newmarket Press, 18 East 48th Street, New York, NY 10017; call (212) 832-3575; fax (212) 832-3629; or e-mail mailbox@newmarketpress.com.

www.newmarketpress.com

Designed by Jaye Medalia

Revised and updated third edition

Manufactured in the United States of America.

b12486310

To all the kids in this world who've had bad breaks. Hang in there—you'll make your own luck.

Contents

Part 1: Business The big picture

Part 2: Business skills Everyday things you have to know to run your business

Part 3: Twenty super businesses
you can start right now

Letter to Kids

Dear Kids,

You might be wondering how a brother and sister—that's us, Arthur and Rose—ended up writing this book. When Arthur was eleven (and Rose was only an infant), he and our mom wrote a book called *The Totally Awesome Money Book for Kids and Their Parents*. It explained how the stock market works, what banks can do for you, how to make a budget, and even how to invest money in other countries.

He traveled all over the United States, to England, and to lots of schools to talk about investing. It was great! Kids learned how to read the stock pages, buy mutual funds, and save for college. Best of all, they liked learning how to buy one share of stock in companies they knew, such as McDonald's, Toys "R" Us, and Burger King.

But many of Arthur's personal friends and kids he met at the schools asked him, "How do I make the money to do all the cool stuff you wrote about in your book?" He thought about that, too. Arthur's answer was always the same: get a job or start a business.

When this book was first written, Arthur was too young to get a job—but not too young to start a business. He did just that, and then wrote about his experience.

If you are curious, his business was selling Magic the Gathering cards through retailers. He bought packs of these collectible cards, sorted them, priced them, and placed them in retail stores in our neighborhood. He earned about thirty to eighty dollars a week, which boiled down to between twenty and sixty dollars after expenses. Today, twenty-five-year-old Arthur works in Washington, D.C., and fifteen-year-old Rose is just starting to find after-school work. But she, too, has learned all about business.

You see, there is a lot to running any business, even a small one like Arthur's. You have to think of a way to make money that works, find people to work with, get supplies, be on time, keep records, speak up for yourself, use the telephone, and do many other big and little tasks.

We think that's what being a business owner (which is also called being an *entrepreneur*) is all about. Adults find that being an entrepreneur is hard to do, but it can actually be very easy for kids like us—and lots of fun. In this book you will learn some skills vital to running a successful business. Of all the things that will be important to you in later life, the most important skill you'll learn is how to see the big picture. More about that later.

After that, you will learn about businesses that you can start right now, including many that can help save the environment. We are very concerned about the environment, and we think most other folks are, too. That's one of the reasons we rewrote this book.

At least ten of the profiled businesses help stop waste or are environmentally sound in other ways. None pollutes the environment. For example, one of the businesses described in this book is bringing some of your recyclable goods to the recycling plant for a profit. Another is a business in which you learn to grow your own plants. With such businesses you can make a profit while helping the environment.

Like our publisher and our mom, we are very interested in getting across ideas about how businesses are formed and how they make money. But of more importance to us is starting out with a worthy idea—an idea that not only works and makes money but also does some good in the world. If nobody is benefiting from what you do and many are harmed, we don't call that business a success, no matter how much money it makes. Doing well by doing good is not just a cliché.

We've also rewritten this book because a lot has changed since it was first published more than ten years ago. The Internet is now even more integrated into the economy, and technology is changing the way *everyone* does business. And now that Rose is one of the authors, she can add a girl's perspective.

If you are worried about getting bored while reading this book, don't be. This book is filled with activities and cartoon characters to keep you interested and entertained as you read. Also, this book is written with kids in mind, so it will be simple to understand.

Before we even start, we can think of three questions you might want to ask already:

1. What's the *big picture* you've been talking about?

The **big picture** is seeing all the important things about a business at once. When we look at a business project, we look at everything. We look at the cost of the business and where we can get the supplies we need to run it successfully. We also look at the way the business would work in our area. We see if the business needs anybody else besides us to make it work. We also look at one of the most important things that a person in business must consider: the skills we need to run the business. In other words, can we do the job?

For instance, if you are going into a baby-sitting business without looking at what skills you may need for the job, you could be in big trouble. What are you going to do if you need to change a diaper but don't know how? What if you need to warm up a bottle but don't know how hot to make it? If you think about such things before starting the business, you could learn how to change a diaper and warm up a bottle, or you could rethink going into this business. So, you see, looking at the big picture is very important.

2. To run some of the businesses in this book, won't I have to work with my parents?

Yes, in many cases, that's true. And for all the businesses, you'll need their permission and cooperation. Yes, we know—yuck. But don't worry. The skill of working with other people, even parents, is called **human relations.** That skill is covered in this book.

You may also have to work with your older or younger brother or sister. That could be even worse! But you must always keep an open mind about the people you are working with. To help you do this, you can think of the rewards you will get if your business is successful.

Arthur worked with our mom for a long time, and now we're working together. So, to give you a head start, we included in this book the things we learned about working with older people.

3. What's the real secret of business success?

As far as we can tell from doing the research for this book and speaking to many successful entrepreneurs, **the biggest secret to success is attitude.** Failure attitudes lead you to fail; success attitudes help you succeed. You need more than just the right attitude; but without it, you can't succeed.

A good attitude shows up right away in your business presentation—that is, in what you call yourself and how you describe and sell your businesses. If you create a clear, specific name for the work you do, such as waste management consultant, you will look like a real expert. People may be more inclined to use your services instead of somebody else's if they understand exactly what it is that you do. This step could be the difference between a successful business and a bad business.

The last word

Before you read this book, you should tell your parents what you are planning—especially if you decide to start a business. This is very important. If you end up doing something your parents don't like, you might get in trouble. Make your parents your partners. Good luck, and enjoy the book.

Letter to Mom and Dad

by Adriane G. Berg

Dear Mom and Dad,

Would you like your children to be masters of their own future? Would you like your children to have fun learning skills that will last a lifetime in career and personal situations? If so, helping and supporting them in starting and running a kid's business will do those very things.

Let me start by acknowledging you for your interest in introducing business concepts early in your child's life. Like any other aspect of parenting, this will take some work on your part, but it will not require that you know much about business yourself. You may learn right along with your child.

For example, you are the target market of some of the businesses outlined in this book. You are the customer. Your participation is required in many ways. You will have to

- $ make demands
- $ complain if you don't like the service
- $ sign contracts
- $ share necessary information
- $ pay on time

In doing these things you will start to think how you conduct business or how your boss or your spouse conducts business. You will have a terrific opportunity to introduce your children to golden values such as integrity, honesty, and responsibility while also helping them develop skills such as public speaking, writing, and math mastery. But your children's most life-framing changes will be in the greater self-esteem and control they will feel when they have run a successful business, even for one fun-filled day.

Before going further, I would like to tell you a little about my background. My father was very educated (as am I), yet he had no idea how to run a business or make a business plan. He died when I was eleven—around the same age Arthur was when we wrote the original *Totally Awesome Money Book for Kids*.

I became interested in money in the way people do when they grow up without any. I believed that getting a good education and becoming an attorney would more than put me in the financial driver's seat. I was wrong. I discovered (I wish it had been sooner) that all people must understand that their jobs, careers, or professions require a good sense of business. In all likelihood, no school will teach your child how to run a business. And if you ever find one that would, then have your child grab the opportunity.

Business is essential to our economic health, as well as our personal wealth. It goes way beyond who we are to what we can do for the world. Your child deserves to understand business. For example, in recent years small businesses have been responsible for more than half of the increase in U.S. employment. Now, women-owned businesses are the fastest-growing business sector. I sit on the board of the Women's Leadership Exchange, and I know how powerful great entrepreneurs can be, no matter how humble their beginnings.

Because I became a financial expert and journalist, I have had the privilege to meet some of the world's most successful businesspeople. I was a guest on the *Oprah* show four times (once with Arthur), and I learned that Oprah Winfrey epitomizes great businesspeople who bring philanthropy to the world. I also coauthored the book *How Good Guys Grow Rich* with Milton Gralla, a global philanthropist. In that book Milton tells how he took $20,000, business know-how, and integrity to create a business that sold for $55 million. Yes, I know the importance of business to personal wealth and to the world's health.

Yet in our culture business has almost become a dirty word. Being a businessperson still does not have the prestige it deserves. We tend to look at business as a separate thing from professions, and not always in complimentary terms. What a pity for our children, who never learn the value and values of business. Even worse, they may get the impression that business is sleazy or beneath them. In fact, we are all in business, and increasing business's level of integrity concerns us all. What better way to start doing that than by addressing the issue in our own home?

Of the twenty businesses described in this book, ten were inspired by Arthur's idea that kids can make money by stopping waste in the home. Since most children are familiar with environmental issues, waste management businesses resonate with them. "Doing well by doing good" is a phrase kids should hear early and often. What a difference that might have made if the Enron and other scandal perpetrators had believed that from their youth.

By the way, *you* will also save a lot of money with the waste management businesses in this book. They really work! I'm not the type who believes you can make a fortune saving soap ends, but I learned from trying these plans with Arthur that this waste management stuff is a powerful savings tool. And what's best, I didn't have to spend a penny's worth of time except to be a good customer and a good sport about changing my terribly wasteful habits...or at least some of them.

There's another good reason kids should learn to handle business right at home. We all know children may face some scary situations if they are working for strangers or in other folks' houses alone. As a mother, I favor safety before revenue, so I'm happy this book focuses on helping children learn about business in their own home.

Although I know a thing or two about business, I am certainly no expert in parenting. Still, parents have always wanted to know my secret in helping Arthur, and later my daughter, Rose (now fifteen years old and the coauthor of this book's current edition), learn about money and business. They have said it in a hundred different ways, but they all have meant it the same way: "How did Arthur learn so much about money?" "How did he get so money-smart?" "How can I best teach my kids to be smarter than I am about money so they won't go through what I go through?" Some have said it right out: "I'd like my kids to be successful on their own when they grow up. How can I help them?"

At first, I shied away from these questions simply because I didn't think I knew the answer. I'm not a teacher or a child psychologist. I'm just another busy parent, like you. Sometimes I feel guilty about how I handle things. Sometimes I feel proud. And sometimes I give up and let my husband handle the mess. And while I don't know more than the next parent, there is one thing I do believe: we make our own luck. I've watched people with good business ideas flounder and blame everyone else for their failure. "Other people have all the luck." "He was born rich." "She married a wealthy hus-band." "If I had what they have, I would be a success." You've probably heard it all before, too. But what can a parent do to show children that they can master their life situations?

It finally came to me, not because of Arthur but because of my then two-year-old Rose Phoebe. When I finally realized the "ultimate secret," it was so simple that I couldn't stretch it out to book length. So, I'll share it with you in a few paragraphs.

During the winter of 1994, our family went to a restaurant for dinner. Rose took off her coat, handed it to the proprietor, helped the waiter bring over a high chair, got into it herself, and ordered soup and rice. The restaurant patrons were stunned at the capability of this little girl. I thought, What's the big deal?

The dinner was the breakthrough. I realized that I expect-ed a lot from my kids because I had (and still have) extreme respect for them. As young children, they were a little short to handle certain things, but they could do a whole lot more than most grown-ups thought possible.

The key, I realized, is to constantly give children situations they can master. The effects snowball. One positive experience leads to another, and one successful endeavor brings on a second, until they have unshakable confidence. Little by little, in bits, they learn.

For example, one aspect of teaching Rose and Arthur about money is including them in many financial discussions, both about our own family and about money in general. I do not shield them, even in rough times. If we have money limitations, they know it. Over time, they have learned that business and financial problems come and go. As a result, they don't get too shaken when they have to face such a problem in their own lives.

Every time you allow your child to handle something, big or small, it reinforces his or her mastery of life's situations. If you need to fly for a business trip, once in a while ask them to help you with arrangements. They learn all about airlines, schedules, and talking to businesspeople. Or, if you need to buy supplies for your office or business, show them how to find suppliers. Think of a few ways right now that you interact with a business and, in turn, of ways you can show effective business interactions to your kids.

And now, the two concepts come together—teaching your child life competence and teaching your child business acumen. I concluded that believing in my children and allowing them to experience success in small increments were keys to helping them toward mastery and success. I'm convinced that once children learn mastery over a hundred little tasks, they'll be able to handle the big stuff themselves.

And now a word from Dad

by Stuart Bochner

There is no question that mastering skills such as keeping records, selling, talking about payment, and setting prices is very important. But, to me, what your children think of themselves while they are learning—what they say to themselves, about themselves—and while they are running a business is more important.

This concept of self-worth, self-appreciation, and self-confidence is the essence of this book. You know what I mean if you have ever seen or heard a youngster say, "I'm no good at math" or "I stink at sports." There they are in the same classroom or gym, receiving the same education and instruction, even doing the same small tasks in increments as all of the other students. And they are not succeeding.

I teach middle and high school students, and I ask myself, "What is it about the children who get great grades in social studies, language arts, and science, yet struggle with math?" It is not intelligence or innate ability. It is their self-evaluation, how they see their relationship to the subject.

A child who says, "I can't," never will. Children who hate a particular subject will reject any notion of success, and will begin a failure spiral by paying less attention and not working hard. The consequence will be a lack of success. That lack of success will lead to less care, work, and attention, and the spiral will deepen.

Now, this is where we, as parents, come in. Children get their ideas about themselves not from us directly but from what they conclude, guess, surmise, or intuit about what we think of them. They may be totally wrong in their opinions or fairly close to correct, but that does not matter. What does matter is that they believe it. And I can prove this.

Just look at yourself. What did your parents think of you? You know, right? Well, did you ever ask them? Probably not. You just reached conclusions. And having done that, you have lived all of your life, both as a child and as an adult, believing—no, knowing—that your assumptions were true. But, surprise! As real as those assumptions appear to be to you, they are, after all, only your guess.

But look at how you have lived your life while believing all of these things. Every time you've said to yourself, "I can't" or "It's not worth it" or "I don't deserve it" or "Why does this always happen to me?" or "This is the way it is for me," you've been experiencing the effects of your conclusions about yourself.

Well, all children follow this pattern: they conclude; they believe; they live. And they are "stuck" with the lives that these conclusions give to them.

So, what can we parents do? The answer is, surprisingly, nothing. We cannot stop our children from concluding things about themselves. They, like everyone else, will inevitably do that. But what we can do is notice. We can be aware of those times in our children's lives when they are being governed or dominated by these arbitrary conclusions. When we see this occurring, we can try to counteract it. We do this by acting like we believe just the opposite. For example, if your child insists that he does not understand math, don't say, "That's okay, since you do so well in all of the other subjects" or, "That's okay, because you can't be good at everything." Instead, point out that he can, if fact, do math. Compliment your children on their achievements; and above all, act as if you know that they can do it. In fact, be as sure they can do it as they are sure they can't. You will be surprised at the result.

But, here is a small warning: this advice can result in a fight between you and your child. He or she may insist, "You don't know me" or "You don't understand." And you will want to prove that you do. Resist this. This is not a war of words but of attitude. You should not try to talk your child out of feeling insecure, but rather go about your life, with your unwavering belief in your child.

Introduction

How to use this book

This is a really easy book to read; but to use it well, you need to do two things: First, take notes on the parts that apply to you and the ways you plan to make money. Second, do your own thinking to make the businesses described in the book work for you.

The book begins with a review of business in general—how it works and what it's really all about. This is useful even if you are not yet ready to start your own business.

Next, a number of special skills, such as using the telephone and the Internet correctly to get information, negotiating, and speaking up for what you want, are discussed. These skills are needed not only in business but also in many things you do each day.

Finally, different kinds of businesses are described. Each section on a suggested business will tell you how much money you can make, how much *capital* (time and money) you need to start the business, the skills you need, and the steps you need to take to make the business work. You also can use your skills and the information in this book to start a business you've thought of yourself. This is how the suggested business sections are set up:

Name of each business

The big picture A description of the business itself.

$-$$$$ The amount of money you stand to make if you start the business. A single dollar sign means the least amount of money you can make; four dollar signs means the most.

Kid's capital The amount you invest, spend, or otherwise put into a business to make money is called **capital.** Most of the time, kid's capital will be time only, not money. But some things, like garage sales, also need paid-for advertising. The best businesses are "low in capital" (do not need much money to start or run), "not labor intensive" (do not need much time to start or run), "cost effective" (you get a profit that is worth the capital you put up).

Skills This tells you what you need to be good at in order to do the job well and make it easy on yourself.

Steps to success This gives you the exact steps you must take to make or save money.

Skills are really what this book is all about

Once you have chosen your favorite business, you'll need the skills to make that business a success. The skills are explained with forms, charts, and ideas to help you make calls, write letters, and even negotiate deals.

We kid-tested every one of these ourselves, and they work. For example, Arthur used to feel shy about making phone calls, but he overcame that feeling by following his own advice. The more he did it, the more comfortable he got. Now he talks to politicians and businesspeople every day. Rose, too, has gotten over her nervousness, and at the age of fifteen is now comfortable talking to any adult.

T	M	I	A	Y	H	E
O						H
C						U
R						R
A						S
E						S
T	W	G	S	I	L	T

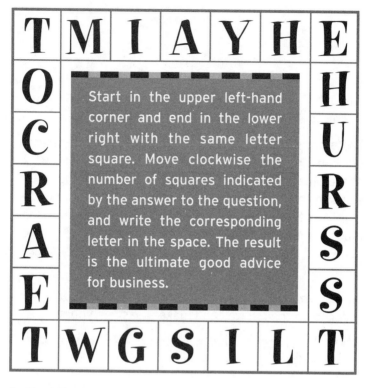

Start in the upper left-hand corner and end in the lower right with the same letter square. Move clockwise the number of squares indicated by the answer to the question, and write the corresponding letter in the space. The result is the ultimate good advice for business.

1. Start T
2. Days in the week __
3. Midnight __
4. Periods in a hockey game __
5. Dime __
6. Twins __
7. Octagon __
8. √25 __
9. Deuce __
10. Great Lakes __
11. Stooges __
12. Pentagon __

13. Solo __
14. Dozen __
15. X __
16. Calling Birds __
17. Blind Mice __
18. Black ball __
19. Stretch inning __
20. Bowling pins __
21. Basketball team __
22. Fortnight __
23. Unlucky __
24. End T

CHAPTER 1

$

An eye for business

What is a business, anyway? When most people think of *business,* they think of companies making money. A company is a thing, an *entity.* But business is really a lot of different things, and different businesses are set up (or structured) in different ways. So, just as there are many different kinds of people, there are many different kinds of businesses. In chapter 2 you will read about many of them and what they can mean for your business.

So one answer to "What is a business?" is that it is a legal entity structured to carry on a trade, service, or production of goods. The entity has its own name, way of doing things, and, some say, personality. Here are the three main types:

$ A business engaged in **trade** is one whose purpose is selling something. It could be a store like Toys "R" Us or a car dealership. These businesses are in the retail trade, which means they sell directly to us, the public. We are the consumers.

Another type of trade or selling business is called **supplying.** Suppliers sell to retailers. For example, Mattel and Nintendo sell to Toys "R" Us.

$ A **service** business sells help, not things. For example, hairdressers, lawyers, doctors, and car mechanics sell their services to you, the consumer.

$ A **producer** of goods manufactures things that trade or service businesses use. For example, Schwinn makes bikes, which bike retail stores sell.

As you will see in chapter 3, the trend today is to have businesses do all three—sell, service, and manufacture. Disney stores are good examples. They manufacture the products that go into the retail stores, they sell products retail (to us), and their service center handles any defects and complaints.

Notice how you knew the names of most of the businesses we just mentioned (Nintendo, Mattel, Disney, etc.)? Well, that's because businesses have their own identifiable names and unique ways of doing things. Advertising folks call this a *brand.* For example, Volkswagen cars advertise a friendly, safe brand. Ben & Jerry's ice cream advertises a laid-back personality. And The Body Shop cosmetics advertise an environmentally conscious personality. When you think of those companies, you think of more than just their names—you think about what the company does and how they do it.

Now, a company's specific brand image doesn't necessarily fit the way the company is actually run. But some companies do act just like their image, and they have employees who do the same.

That brings us to another aspect of "What is a business?" A business is an idea held by the people who create and start the business.

Who was the first person to do business? Maybe a caveman who was weak and couldn't find his own food but knew where the animals were. Maybe he offered to tell where the animals were in return for a portion of some hunter's food. Funny to think that business could have started with weakness, but it's probably true. After all, if we could all do everything for ourselves all the time, we wouldn't need help from others. When others help us and get something in return, they are in business! However doing business actually began, we love that caveman because he didn't just give up. He took his strength (knowing where the animals were), combined it with a good idea, and turned them into a business.

That's an important point. A business must start with a good idea that helps you and others. In chapter 3, you'll read about ideas such as manufacturing and retailing that make a business great. They are called the *business purpose.*

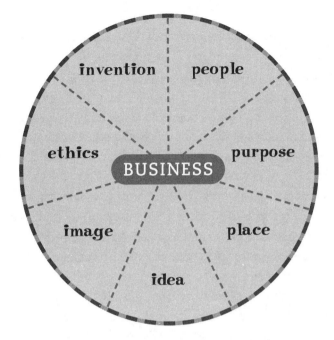

When some people think of a business, they think of a place. Our great-grandmother, a woman who worked many years before the majority of women worked outside the home, used to say, "I'm going to business." To her, the store where she sold jewelry was business itself.

Today, designing office buildings, plants that manufacture goods, industrial parks, and office spaces is itself a business—and a very important one to all other businesses. After all, even our caveman needed a convenient rock where hunters could find him. In chapter 4, you will read about places of business. One of the most modern business locations is the home office, which uses the *information superhighway* (computers and telecommunications).

For us, the most important answer to "What is business?" is *people*. Without people, there is no business. And if robots could run a business by themselves, there would be no purpose to it anyway.

A business is all the people who work to make it run. That includes the owners of the business, the secretaries, the managers at all levels, and lots more. In chapter 5, we describe the people who work in businesses.

At the end of this book you will be able to take on the role of a special type of worker: the consultant—a professional who gives advice or provides services to make other people's lives, homes, or businesses more effective, efficient, or profitable.

We know that businesses have a body (a legal entity), a personality (a brand image), a goal (business purpose), and a heart (its people). But does business have a conscience? Does business know right from wrong? Today, the answer to this question is called *business ethics*. We cover this subject in chapter 6 so you can think about it before you go into business yourself.

The body of a business

Corporations, partnerships, and sole proprietorships

Businesses have their own separate names; they file their own tax returns; they even have their own addresses. And businesses can live on even after the owner of a business dies. Spooky!

The first car company, Ford Motor, is one example. It was started by Henry Ford in 1903 and is still manufacturing and selling cars today. But you don't have to look to the past to find examples of businesses that have lived on after their founder has gone.

You can see plenty of examples just by watching television. Watch the new Orville Redenbacher popcorn ads. You'll see old images of him, old commercials in fact, that evoke the company's history. The chicken man, Jim Perdue, is on TV—and guess what? His dad, Frank, was the chicken man when Arthur was a kid (in fact, Jim Perdue is the third generation of Perdues to run that company). Daughters, too, like Marcy Syms of the famous discount clothing stores Syms, are in on the act. In the Syms ads, Marcy looks at the camera, just like her father did, and assures us that an educated consumer is her best customer. Some companies—and their customers—value tradition.

A business has a life of its own because it is set up in special ways and registered, usually under government regulations. There are many types of business entities, and more types are being created. Internet businesses are growing faster and faster, and the government is just now getting around to regulating them.

But today, the three most common types of business entities are the corporation, the partnership, and the sole proprietorship.

Corporations

A *corporation* is a business entity in which *stock,* or shares of ownership in that corporation, are issued. The holders of those stocks are the true owners of the corporation. If you owned all the shares, you would own the whole corporation—its inventory, profits, leases, and everything else it had. When only a few people own all the shares in a corporation and the shares can't be sold to just anyone else *(restricted shares)*, it's called a *closed corporation*. Many family-owned businesses are like that. In our other book, *The Totally Awesome Money Book for Kids (and Their Parents)*, we discuss a different kind of corporation called a *public corporation*. Public corporations include PepsiCo, McDonald's, Mattel, Toys "R" Us, and hundreds more. That kind of company sells shares to the public. If you own a share, you are part owner of the corporation.

To form a corporation, people must have a business idea or purpose. They must put it in writing and file a business certificate in the state where they have a business home. That is called their *state of incorporation*. Once the certificate is accepted, the company is alive! It gets a registered name and applies for a tax identification number (that's a lot like your Social Security number). With it, the corporation can open bank accounts, sign contracts, and carry out just about every other business transaction done by individuals.

Of course, the corporation needs real people to think for it and actually sign its name. They are called its *officers* and *directors*. Some small companies have only one person as an officer and director, as with our mom, who says she wears many hats. She is the president, vice-president, treasurer, secretary, and all the other officers and directors of her company. The good part is that when she calls a meeting, everybody arrives on time.

Large corporations, the type you buy shares in, usually have many officers and directors. The chief executive officer, or CEO, has one of the most powerful and best-paid jobs in the world. A CEO runs the entire company, does the hiring, and makes the big business decisions. But the CEO usually doesn't own the corporation—the shareholders do. Another powerful corporate person is the chief financial officer, CFO, who handles the money for the corporation. The CEO and the CFO are still only employees of the company and, therefore, of the shareholders. They get a salary for their work. Sometimes, as part of their compensation, they get shares of stock in the company, so they are shareholders, too. So if you have a share in a company, even its high-paid CEO or CFO works for you.

Partnerships

Another type of legal entity is the *partnership,* in which two or more people are the owners. No shares are issued. To be an owner, you must make a deal, usually, but not always, with a written contract. People become partners for many reasons. They may be in the same family and want to work together. They may need to hire someone and can't afford to, so they share the business with someone else. Or they may find someone who can offer much that is compatible with what they have to offer.

For example, let's say the caveman who knows where to find the food notices that one hunter brings back more than the rest. He says, "Let's be partners. I'll tell you where the food is, you catch it, and we'll sell it to the other cavemen."

"Why should we do that?" says the hunter, "What's in it for us?" "Well," says the caveman, "we don't have time to gather fruits and berries. We could exchange meat for fruits and berries and have both that way." "Swell idea," says the hunter. "Let's be partners."

We don't want to make partnership arrangements sound too easy. It's hard to find good people to work with whom you like. Also, you really must know how to be fair and to share the labor and the profits so each person is happy. That's why most partnerships have a partnership agreement that spells out the rules the partners will abide by.

Many of the businesses in this book can be structured as a partnership with one of your friends. Write up an agreement that includes

§ **who does** what

§ **who brings** what to the business

§ **who gets** what

§ **how the profits** and other stuff the business owns are to be divided if you go out of business

If one of you gives money to the business to buy supplies and the other gives extra time and works more, make sure the way you divide the profits is fair. What is fair? Every partner has a different view. That's one place Skill 6, negotiating, will come in handy.

Today, most partnerships are used by medium-size companies, as well as by doctors, lawyers, and other professionals.

Sole proprietorships

A *sole proprietorship* is the easiest of all business entities to start. One (sole) person (proprietor) owns and runs everything. The proprietor may hire employees, but only she or he owns the business. Usually, these are the smallest companies in terms of moneymaking, but not always. As kids, you will probably be sole proprietors. Many sole proprietorships grow and become partnerships with one or more partners. Others incorporate and sell shares.

Some of these corporations *go public,* or begin to sell on the stock exchange, and you can buy stock in them. A good example of this is the Celestial Seasonings Company, which began with a sole proprietor picking herbs to make tea. Another example is Weight Watchers, which began with one woman holding meetings in her living room to help her friends lose weight.

Our mom was one of the lawyers for Weight Watchers, and she also met the owners of Celestial Seasonings on a few television shows where they both talked about business. My mom says that these business owners made it big for lots of reasons that all came together. First, they picked businesses that people really wanted to use. Herbal teas were just right for the health-conscious baby boomers. Diets are always important businesses in overweight America. But, there was more to it than that.

Each of these companies was started by someone who believed in the business and was passionate about it. Those folks really felt what they were doing was good for everyone, fun to do, and helpful to the world. They were willing to work very hard because of this passion. What do you have a passion for? If you figure that out, we bet your business won't be far behind.

Some people say that business is what makes the United States great. They say that it's a big reason people come from all over the world to live here. We agree. But we also think it's fun to own your own business. It's creative, like painting a picture or writing a song.

Which brings us to the "business idea."

CHAPTER 3

The mind of a business

Business purpose and idea

> You can go a long way with the right idea!

Sensible Steve

Having a piece of paper such as a certificate of incorporation or a partnership agreement doesn't necessarily mean you have a business. You need an idea that lives, too—a purpose to what you are doing and for which you hope to get money. All businesses can be divided up by their purpose. If the purpose is a good one and the idea behind it is smart, you will probably have a successful business.

In fact, the mind of a business can be much more important than its body. A good purpose and idea can help you make money whether you have a corporation, a partnership, or a sole proprietorship.

Here are some of the top business purposes:

- **$** **Gathering raw materials** (mining for metals, drilling for gas, cutting lumber) to be used in manufacturing

- **$** **Supplying** (selling raw materials to the manufacturers)

- **$** **Manufacturing** (making things that people need)

- **$** **Wholesaling** (selling manufactured goods to the retailers)

- **$** **Retailing** (selling manufactured goods to the public)

- **$** **Consulting** (advising other people or businesses about how to do any part of their business better)

- **$** **Servicing** (providing any kind of service, such as legal, secretarial, cleaning, or moving, to people or businesses)

- **$** **Telecommunications** (providing electronic means of talking or otherwise getting messages to companies and people)

- **$** **Construction** (building homes, roads, bridges, and all types of buildings)

Notice something interesting about these business purposes? Doctors and cleaning services are lumped together; manufacturing airplanes and manufacturing blue jeans are in the same category. Purposes may be the same in small and big business, as well as in businesses that take lots of skill and those that don't. Businesses with the same purpose can look very different. For example, when Arthur thinks of manufacturing, he thinks about the Boeing airplanes he once saw being produced in Seattle and about the garment-center employees he'd often seen pushing racks of freshly made clothes down Manhattan's Seventh Avenue. Although different in size and product, both Boeing and the garment workers' employers are manufacturers.

Here are some businesses.
In which category do you think each falls?

__**a.** Singer

__**b.** Automobile production

__**c.** Timber cutting

__**d.** House building

__**e.** Gold mining

__**f.** Telephone service

__**g.** Soda bottling

Answers:
a. Servicing
b. Manufacturing
c. Raw materials
d. Construction
e. Raw materials
f. Telecommunication
g. Wholesaling

Today, many people say we are in a postindustrial society. That means all the categories of businesses (industries) have already cropped up, and we are now going beyond industry to a world where information gathering will be our most important business purpose. But it was only 150 years ago when we were still in a time called the *Industrial Revolution*. People were trying to invent machines that helped with the manufacture of many things. Here are just a few famous inventors and their dream machines:

1794: Eli Whitney, the cotton gin

1831: Cyrus McCormick, the reaper

1879: Thomas A. Edison, the electric lightbulb

Today, many inventors are making new microchips and better semiconductors.

No matter how advanced business gets, one thing we do know is that all businesses need other businesses in other categories. Just as people depend on one another, most businesses can't get along without one another, either.

As we discussed in chapter 1, business, by definition, can have three purposes: trade, service, and manufacturing. Trade is selling, service is helping, and manufacturing is making things. As you can see, the sellers need the manufacturers, or they would have nothing to sell. The manufacturers need the traders, or no one would sell their goods. The service people either repair the goods if something goes wrong or provide other services that can be done only through human effort, like fixing the plumbing or telling jokes. So the

- $ **service business** (shop-window designer) needs the
- $ **retailer** (shop owner), who needs the
- $ **wholesaler** (seller of goods), who needs the
- $ **manufacturer** (maker of goods), who needs the
- $ **supplier** of raw materials (cotton merchant), who needs the
- $ **raw materials** (cotton).
- $ And they all use **telecommunications** in order to make their work easier.

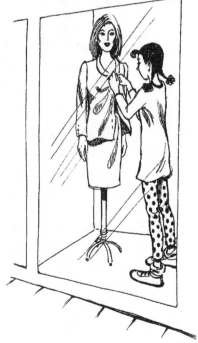

That's the business circle of interdependency!

Write down some of your great business ideas. In which categories do they fall? Which other businesses will you need to make yours work?

CHAPTER 4
$

The home of a business

Office, factory, industrial park, house

Of all a business's aspects, its home is the easiest to understand because we can see it—at least for now. Many of us have visited our mother's or father's office. Maybe our grandparents', too. This often is where the personality of a business shows up clearly. Some offices are huge; others are tiny. Some are full of state-of-the-art high-tech equipment, and others have just a computer.

Of course, retail businesses have stores; and whether it's a butcher shop or a big department store, the store is home for the business. But some of the biggest retail businesses have no stores. They sell through catalogs, TV shopping networks, or the Internet. Those retail businesses have a home, too, although it's usually an office building their customers never see.

HOME OF A BUSINESS

Until our family moved to New Jersey, Rose had never seen a *commercial park,* or college campus–type place where smaller businesses share space. One near us has a hotel, a day-care center, an emergency room, and artificial lawns that look like golf courses. (Office design is a business in itself that you might want to go into one day.)

Factories are also homes for businesses, and factories have changed a lot over the years. Many old-fashioned factories have been replaced by new ones with state-of-the-art machinery that helps do work faster and more efficiently. But some new machines replace people with robots. That's another part of our postindustrial world. Routine factory jobs are being eliminated in favor of machines doing the work. The machines might make the factory more efficient and profitable (and make the products they produce cheaper for consumers), but factory workers and their families can be hurt when such changes occur. Businesses have growing pains just like kids—and those pains can be rough.

It's hard to talk about something as seemingly simple as a factory without getting into important issues. Should we slow manufacturing progress and reduce profitability to save people's jobs? Should we use more machines that would reduce production costs, so that goods would be cheaper and poor people could buy more of the things they need? As you can see, discussing factories and manufacturing leads us to big, tough issues—ones you might be helping to solve someday.

Another interesting thing about the place of business is that it may be headed back to the home. In the 1700s, before the Industrial Revolution, most places of business were on farms and in homes. When manufacturing began, the new machines, such as looms and sewing machines, were operated right in the house. These businesses were called *cottage industries*.

In the 1800s, factories were built during what is known as the Industrial Revolution. The Smithsonian Institution, headquartered in Washington, D.C., has an exhibit that features these factories and machines. They are beautiful, very old-fashioned, and unfamiliar. By the 1950s, office buildings, sleek factories, and industrial parks housed a lot of businesses and took up a lot of space. They still do, and more people work there than in their homes.

But there is another revolution. Because of computers and telecommunications, people are starting to work from home again. Millions of Americans are *telecommuting*. They work for a company, but they work at home and communicate through computers and phones.

We have an example at home. Our mom is also a writer, and she used to publish a newsletter. She used a printing company, a company that takes orders, an 800-number phone company, a credit card company, and a fulfillment house that put postage on the newsletter and mailed it out. She never actually saw the homes of any of these companies. In fact, they were all in other states, and they all communicated by computer and phone. Our mother's only equipment was a three-pound computer that she carried in a backpack. You could say our mom's place of business was her backpack!

When you select the business you want to start, come back to this chapter and think about your ideal business home.

The heart of a business

People

More than ever, we are learning that people are the heart of business. At first, the owners of businesses believed that the people who worked there were not at all important. Child labor, low wages, and horrible working conditions were all part of the Industrial Revolution. But things changed. Labor unions, strikes, and even violence are all part of business history. A *labor union* is like a club in which workers can join together to make their employer deal with them as a group, rather than as individuals.

This gives the employees more power. One way to use this power is for everyone to stop working all at once until the employer gives them what they want. When workers stop working, it's called *going on strike.*

There are both state and federal fair labor laws with which business must comply. There are labor-management contracts that can be enforced in the courts and at special hearings called *arbitrations.*

Today, there are different issues about people in business. Many of those issues involve fair hiring practices, or efforts to make sure that members of minority groups, women, older people, and others aren't discriminated against in hiring.

Not everyone agrees on what is fair. Many say that businesses work best when they are run by all types of folks, each bringing new ideas and ways of doing things. Others feel that government and unions have no right to dictate so many rules to business, and that what's good for one group may become unfair to another.

What do you think? Is *affirmative action*—requiring businesses to hire certain people, such as minority members and women, who were excluded from working in the past—a good idea or not? Or should all hiring be based solely on a person's ability to do the job?

How about allowing U.S. businesses to use workers from other countries where they can be paid only a few pennies an hour, where children are still put to work, and where there can be terrible workplace conditions in places often called sweatshops?

These are hard questions. Talk to your parents about them.

When we do, there are always lots of very loud discussions about whether business does best when it's free to do as it likes or whether it needs regulation. Our father once worked as a labor lawyer, and he dealt with both labor and management. Boy, does he have ideas on the subject!

Ways businesses use personnel

No matter what their politics, most people still agree that people are the heart of a business. If you look at the different things that people do in a business, the roles they can play, you can get an idea of what jobs you would like to fill, even if you don't yet have a business of your own.

Here are some ways businesses use their *personnel* (employees).

Upper management

- Ⓢ Officers (president, vice-president, treasurer)
- Ⓢ Directors

These people make top decisions about the business as a whole. For example, they would decide how much to manufacture, what line of toys would be sold at Christmas, and what advertising style should mark the business's *brand image*.

Middle management

- Ⓢ Department heads
- Ⓢ Vice-presidents (sometimes)

These people carry out the decisions of upper management and make decisions of their own regarding how to get things done. They also supervise the support staff.

Support staff

$ Secretaries

$ Receptionists

$ Administrators

$ Bookkeepers

$ Computer operators

$ Factory workers

$ And just about anybody else who is not management

As you can imagine, each company is very different when it comes to its workers. In some small businesses, the owner (upper management) does his or her own typing. In other businesses, there may be a very powerful vice-president in charge of marketing a product. In other industries, such as banking, lots of people are given the title of vice-president, but many of them are not in upper management at all.

So the one thing we've learned is not to be fooled by titles on a business card. But, of course, most people *do* care what their title is—and they should. They feel better as vice-president of interoffice communications than they do as mail room attendant.

Productive and happy workers

More and more businesses are learning that they do better and are more productive (make more money) when their workers are happy. Using clear job titles that people like and having clear chains of command are good starting points. Today, there is a trend toward flexible schedules for working

Make up fancy names for these jobs:

Teacher_____

Lawyer_____

Janitor_____

Computer operator_____

Author_____

Garbage collector_____

Nurse_____

Manicurist _____

Cook_____

Assembly-line auto worker_____

mothers, stress-release sessions, and gyms in the workplace. Telecommuting is also a big new part of making workers happier.

America has come a long way from the days of sweatshops and child labor. Many other countries in the world have far to go to catch up to our standards. We may have many faults, but after reading about working conditions in other countries for this book, we are very proud of the United States and our high standards.

That brings us to the chapter on the conscience of a business.

$

The conscience of a business

Business ethics

Good business is good for people, too.

Pablo Payment

usinesses are a lot like people. They can't just do anything they want. They can't cheat you, pollute rivers, or make medicines that harm you. They are under a lot of regulation, mostly from the federal government.

CONSCIENCE OF A BUSINESS

This is not a book on politics, but it's hard to write about business today without mentioning Washington, D.C. There are vast differences of opinion about how much control the government should have over business. Some say none at all—just let people stop using a business if they don't like it; then it will "go out of business." People who feel this way are sometimes called *conservatives*. Others feel that the government is needed to protect us from bad business practices. People who feel this way are sometimes called *liberals*. Arthur works in Washington and deals with both groups every day.

The main question that we, as business kids, have to ask ourselves is whether we think a business has an obligation to do the right thing even if it means making less profit. Everyone agrees that the goal of every business is to make more money than it takes to run the operation. If lots more is made, it's a good business. If only a little more is made, the business is called *marginal*. If it costs more to run than it makes, the business will eventually fail.

But what if profits can be made by cutting the quality of the raw materials used or by importing cheap labor? Does a business have a duty to make less money, maybe pay some of its top people less, or even go out of business instead of cutting corners?

If you think these are tough questions, what about this one? Does a business have the obligation not to manufacture or sell something the public wants because it's no good for the public? Examples of this are cigarettes, alcohol, and fatty foods. What about animal testing for medical research? Some

people think it's wrong; others think it's okay because it saves human lives. What about fast food? It can be very unhealthy, but most people eat it anyway, even though they know about its problems. Should fast-food companies be prohibited from making money (often millions!) by making people unhealthy, or should fast-food companies be allowed to sell whatever they want? We love the idea of going into business; and if you've gotten this far into the book, you probably do, too. Our own view is that government regulates business too much. Paperwork and taxes can stop a lot of good businesses before they even get started. But lots of government regulations were developed years ago because of businesses that were only out for profit and didn't show a conscience. Today, businesses are different (mostly), and we are a new generation of businesspeople. We know better, and have learned a lot from the bad ethics of the leadership at Enron and other companies that have recently been dishonest. Maybe if we do better, the government won't tell us what to do.

PART 2

Business skills:

Everyday things you have to know to run your business

Skill 1:
Speaking up

You can really go far if you let your voice be heard.

Arnold Almost Adult

Why don't most people speak up about problems?

1. **People don't think speaking up** is worth the effort.

2. **People don't know how** or where to complain.

3. **People don't believe** speaking up will do any good.

4. **People are afraid** that they will get yelled at or laughed at when they speak up, and they don't want to get their feelings hurt.

All these reasons that people are afraid of speaking up are, for the most part, mistaken. It is worth the effort; it will do good; and it is easy to learn how and whom to talk to. In business, you must be able to communicate!

Why you should speak up

Complaining is not that hard if you actually have a problem. If you don't have a real one, then you will get laughed at or ignored. And complaining just to make others feel bad or get them in trouble doesn't work.

But when you do have a real problem, you should not be afraid to speak up. There's a good chance you will get results if you do, and no chance if you don't. Results-oriented complaining works. Sometimes you can even change the world by complaining. You should speak up when you have a problem with service or prices, or when you experience any other injustice.

How you can speak up

This is how to speak up effectively: If the issue is something simple, as when you feel you were not charged the right price at the supermarket, you can start out with, "Excuse me, I think you didn't charge me the price marked on the item's price tag." That will usually work.

If the issue is something more complicated, like a problem with your phone bill, you might want to provide more proof, such as showing the incorrect bill. Most of the time, people don't get what they want because they don't know how to get it. When you call up to complain, always have a solution and a date by which you want results.

Sometimes you may need to speak up about something that's not a problem. For instance, you may want to call for a favor such as a price break. When you do, be ready to negotiate in order to get what you want.

If you are especially good at speaking up, you can join a lobbying group. A *lobbying group* is a group of people who speak to people high in our government about a certain issue that they have a strong opinion about.

Who you should talk to

If you are speaking up about something, you need to make sure you talk to someone who can really help you, not someone in the wrong department or someone who isn't allowed to make decisions. When you have a problem, you usually should speak to the person in charge of the company or business that did you wrong. Find the person with the most power. Remember, you'll always get a no if the person you're talking to doesn't have the power to say yes. And, of course, always be polite! If you need to speak with someone different from the person you're talking to, ask nicely—if you're rude or mean, you won't get passed on to the right person.

When you should speak up

When you experience a problem, you should complain immediately, instead of letting the complaint get old. The best time to complain is during the week (but not on a Friday), rather than on weekends. There are two good times to call during the day: first thing in the morning and right after

Almost 70 percent of people with consumer problems don't complain. Too bad, because 40 percent of people who took action were satisfied with the results. (See the Gripe Book.)

Responsible Rhoda

the people you are going to complain to get back from their lunch break.

What to do if you don't get results

If you don't get results the first time you complain, you should try again. You will probably get results the second time. There are other things you can do if you can't get results by calling the company you are having the problem with. There are many places that can help you: the Better Business Bureau, Call for Action, your local radio station, and even your congressperson. You can also contact government agencies. See the list in *The Great American Gripe Book,* by Matthew Lesko (listed on page 181).

Don't forget to put everything in writing. As soon as you speak to someone, write a letter that confirms either the offer to help or the refusal to do so. Send it to the person you spoke to, and send a copy to his or her boss. Be sure to give a date by which you want results.

CHAPTER 8

Skill 2: Making business budgets

Everyone needs a budget in business.

Barry Budgeter

What is a business budget?

A *business budget* is a way of figuring out whether you are making or losing money in your business. A budget is a must if you are in business.

Budget versus cash flow

Cash flow is the "time" when you receive and spend money. Sometimes you spend and get paid at the same time; sometimes, at different times. If you have to spend before the money comes in, you have a *cash flow problem.*

When you make a business budget, you must take cash flow into account. Even if you make more money each month than you spend, you still may get a bill that you cannot pay on time because your cash has not come in yet. You should always make sure that you have cash so that you can pay a bill anytime it may come in.

How to make a budget

Budgeting is not that hard after you do it a few times. In general, this is how you make a budget: Write down all the things that you make money *(income)* from. Then write down how much money you make from each item. Next, total up the money that you make. The next step is to do the

Cash Flow

Income		Expenses	
1. Farm sale, May 30	$10.00	1. Plastic bags, June 1	$7.00
2. Farm sale, June 5	$10.00	2. Ribbons, June 1	$3.00
3. Farm sale, July 5	$10.00	3. Worms, June 6	$4.00
Total	$30.00	Total	$14.00

same thing with your expenses. Finally, subtract the expenses from the income. If there is money left over, you are doing very well. If the result is zero, you have a balanced budget. But if the expenses are greater than the income, you are in trouble and have to reduce spending or increase income.

Working with a business budget

A business budget is exactly the same as a regular personal or household budget, except it keeps track of the income you get from your business and the money you spend *(expenses)* on that business (and not your home expenses, allowance, etc.). Here is Rose's budget for an old business of hers, Rose's Good Garbage. She sold compost, as described in Business 6 (chapter 18):

Rose's Business Budget: May 30 to August 15

EXPENSES:		INCOME:		
ITEM	COST	Sale	May 30	$10.00
Plastic bags	$7.00	Sale	June 5	$10.00
Ribbons	$3.00	Sale	July 5	$10.00
Worms	$4.00	TOTAL	$30.00	
TOTAL	$14.00			

TOTAL INCOME	$30.00
TOTAL COSTS	$14.00
PROFIT OVER 6 WEEKS	$16.00

Why should you budget?

You should budget because if you do, you will know whether you have a good business or a bad one. When you budget, you should always make sure that you are writing the correct numbers down; otherwise, you will think that your business is either doing badly when it's really doing well or, instead, doing well when it's actually not.

If you don't budget, you might

💲 work without making money

💲 never realize how good your business is and not expand

💲 not know how to cut costs

💲 not know if you are charging enough for your work

Here is a sample budget for you to fill out. Try it before you start a business. It will help you decide if it's a good one.

INCOME:	EXPENSES:
allowance: $_____	business expenses: $_____
gifts: $_____	things you want to spend on: $_____
business income: $_____	lunch: $_____
odd jobs: $_____	charity: $_____
other income: $_____	**TOTAL EXPENSES:** $_____
TOTAL INCOME: $_____	**TOTAL INCOME:** $_____
	minus total expenses: $_____
	EQUALS: $_____

Arthur's totally awesome hobby/business

When I was in middle school, I started to play a game called Magic the Gathering. It is a card game somewhat like Dungeons and Dragons, and it is still being played today. The company that makes the cards for this game did not make enough to meet the demands of players. A lot of kids liked this game, and the stores couldn't get enough cards to sell to them. So, I thought that I could make money by selling some of my cards to kids through the local card store in my town. I opened packs and kept the cards I wanted. I took those cards I didn't want to the card store, where they were sold for me. The store got 30 percent of whatever they sold, and I got 70 percent. I got back the cards they didn't sell. The purpose of my business was being a supplier. Here are a time sheet, a profit/loss statement, an income sheet, and an expense sheet related to my business.

How are you doing?

$ I have money to spare. I'm doing great.

$ I need to spend less.

$ I'm balanced.

Don't be afraid of a budget

Some people don't budget because they are afraid that a budget will limit them and keep them from getting what they

BUSINESS BUDGETS

Expense Sheet—Weekly

Card packs	$35.00
Transportation	$1.00
Packaging	$10.00
Total Cost:	**$46.00**

Income Sheet—Weekly

Income from store (average)	$100.00
Total:	**$100.00**

Profit/Loss Statements—Weekly

Income per week	$100.00
Expenses per week	$46.00
Profit:	**$54.00**

Time Sheet—Weekly

Hours worked:

1 hour per day, 7 days a week = 7 hours a week

Profit = $54.00

Profit divided by hours worked = (54 ÷ 7) = $7.71

I made $7.71 an hour

want. It's not true. Budgets, whether business or personal ones, are the only way to set and achieve financial goals.

One of the biggest reasons people go out of business is that they don't have enough capital to start or keep up a business. If they made a budget to begin with, they would know what they were in for before starting. This is called a *preliminary budget*. Do one now for a business that interests you.

Here's some math that will help you make a budget.

Averages

To find the average of something, you have to add all the numbers together, then divide the total sum by the number of numbers you added together. For example, suppose that you made $15 one week, $20 the next week, and $18 the third week, and you wanted to find out the average of your earnings for those weeks. First, you add all of your earnings together. You will get a total of $53. You then divide that total by 3 because you added 3 numbers together to get $53. You then get $17.66. That is the average amount of money you made per week.

Percentages

To find a percentage of something, you have to divide the second number by the first number. For example, suppose you had 80 baseball cards, 10 of which were Yankee cards. If you wanted to find out what percentage of your cards were Yankee cards, you would divide 10 by 80 (10÷80 = 0.13). Since all percentages are based on 100, you would then multiply 0.13 by 100 to get the percentage. So, 13 percent of your cards are Yankee cards (0.13 x 100 = 13%).

Skill 3: Record keeping and filing

You might need file cards, file folders, envelopes, and labels.

Marvin Mogul

The importance of records

Records are the life of your business. Without them, you don't know what you have to do next, and you can't keep track of what you have already done for your business. Records serve many purposes.

They tell you

1. what people owe you (**accounts receivable**)

2. how much people have paid you already (**income**)

3. how much you owe others (**accounts payable**)

4. how much you have paid others (**expenses**)

5. **business budget**

6. **suppliers' names** and addresses

7. **customers' names** and addresses

If you were going into the garage-sale business, for example, you might also keep records of

1. **what you have sold**

2. **how much you sold** those items for

3. **how many people** came to your sale

4. **how many pieces** of merchandise you brought to the sale and didn't end up selling

Profit-and-loss records

A *profit-and-loss* record is the last part of your business budget. Just take the total income and subtract the total expenses. You get your profit or loss for the month. After about three months, you can tell how your business is doing. If after a while there is a big change, you may be doing something different that is causing the change. It could be good (a bigger profit) or bad (a smaller profit or a loss). The statement keeps you alert to business change so you can do more of the good stuff and fix the bad.

Time sheets

We learned about *time sheets* from our parents, who are both lawyers. Lawyers are mostly paid for their time at an hourly rate. They have to prove to their clients how much time they spent on a case so they can get paid. As a waste consultant (one of the businesses in this book), you may be paid by the hour, too, and need to keep time records. But mostly you will be paid with a cut (a portion) of the money saved. Still, time records are very important for a consultant. You will always be using your time as your capital. Keep records of how much time you spend each day at your business:

Date:____   Job:_____   Hours:_____

____   _____   _____

____   _____   _____

By knowing how much money you made in your business through the profit-and-loss records, you can figure out how much you earned per hour. Just divide the profit for the month by the time for the month:

$$\frac{\text{Profit}}{\text{Time}} = \frac{\$20.00}{4 \text{ hours}} = \$5.00 \text{ per hour}$$

You can then compare what you earned with something that pays strictly by the hour, like baby-sitting. In most places, the minimum wage for grown-ups is $5.15 per hour. (Congress is now debating about whether to raise that amount, and by the time you read this book, the minimum wage could be higher.) How is your business doing compared with the minimum wage?

Filing

After you know what records you need, you must set up a *filing system*. You can use programs on your computer (such as Excel, Word, and Access). If you keep paper records, try to use envelopes because papers can easily fall out of open file folders. Files with tie strings are big and expensive. Instead, use 8½-by-11-inch envelopes that close with a metal fastener. To keep track of what's inside each envelope, write the date and title of each paper on a top sheet that you keep in—or stapled to—the envelope. Keep the envelopes in alphabetical order, inside a desk drawer or other safe place. Here's a list before and after it's been alphabetized:

Unalphabetized list of files	Alphabetized list of files
Smith	Carson
Jones	Jackson
Samson	Jones
Jackson	Samson
Carson	Smith

How to alphabetize

To alphabetize, you organize using the first letter of the file. *A* comes before *B,* and so on. If the files have the same first letter, just go to the second letter. For instance, in the list you just saw, the *Ja* of *Jackson* would come before the *Jo* of *Jones.* Choose the system that works best for you. But file every day, or else all the information that's coming in will get out of hand, and you'll never find anything.

CHAPTER 10
$

Skill 4: Communicating- Telephoning & e-mailing

Don't be intimidated

Being able to communicate is a key skill in any business. When you're on the phone with an adult, do not be afraid to talk. Speak up. If the adult you are talking to giggles or laughs, it's not to make you embarrassed. He's probably just giggling because he is flabbergasted that you are acting so professionally. When you are talking, never feel that the adult you're talking to is trying to get you off the phone.

Speak slowly

Whenever you are talking on the phone, always speak slowly and clearly. You should do that even when you're not on the phone with adults. Always make sure that you don't drop your voice at the end of a sentence or a word. When you speak, always make sure that the adult doesn't have to say "What?" all the time.

What if the adult doesn't want to talk to you?

If the adult you are trying to reach doesn't want to talk to you, you should say exactly why you are calling. Adults will want to talk to you if they know you have a serious purpose and are not wasting their time. It's good to say something nice to them like, "Your job at the telephone company must be pretty interesting," or, "Everyone said that you would have the right information for me."

If the person you want to speak to isn't in his or her office, is on vacation, or is in a meeting, you should leave a message saying the time that you called, your name, your number, and the reason for your call. Also mention when it would be a good time for that person to call you back.

Take notes

When you talk on the phone about a business matter, you should always have a pen or pencil and a piece of paper so you can take notes. When you're on the phone, it's important to take notes in case you forget anything that you talked about during the conversation. Make a note of whom you called, why you called, when you called, and whom you should call next or what you should do next. Write down the information you got, any numbers you might need for the future, and the best time to call again if you need to.

E-mailing

Writing a business e-mail is just as serious as making a business phone call. Your e-mail should be polite, professional, and free of any grammatical mistakes. Even though you might use shorthand or slang in your e-mails, text, and instant messages to your friends, you shouldn't do so when you're writing about business. For instance, don't write "C U next 2sday" when you want to say "see you next Tuesday." Adults want to know that you are a professional.

Just as with telephone calls, be careful whom you are e-mailing and what information you give them! Not everyone has good intentions. In fact, you should check with your parents before e-mailing someone or giving out any information by e-mail or over the phone. Be especially careful about giving any of your personal or business information to anyone you don't already know and trust.

Always follow up

Whenever you are making calls about a business matter, you should always make sure that you follow up. After you have talked to somebody who has told you to call someone else for more information, you should always do it. Never leave a job half done.

CHAPTER 11
$

Skill 5:
Using the telephone book & Internet to get information

My fingers do the sorting.

Sensible Steve

Alphabetize the possibilities

F inding information is critical to doing good business. Whether you use the telephone book or the Internet, make sure you know how and where to get the best information.

When you use a phone book, the things you look up are in alphabetical order (just like your files, we hope), with words following the alphabet, from *A* to *Z*. As mentioned before, if two or more words start with the same letter, you should go on to the next letter. For example, the last name *Baker* would come before *Bochner,* since *Ba* would come before *Bo*.

What the telephone book can do for you

Telephone books contain an amazing amount of information! As we discuss more in a moment, their information is divided into several sections, to make it easier for people to find what they need. In the white pages, you can find a listing of businesses in your area. If you have blue pages, those will list all federal, state, county, and local government offices in your area. The yellow pages can tell you the products and services available in your area. This is where you can look up restaurants or movie theaters, for example. You will also find your local gas, power, and light companies listed in the yellow pages.

You can also find a list of zip codes for your state so you can address your business letters properly, and you often can find such things as diagrams of local sports arenas. Also, there often are maps showing the location of parks, area attractions, and museums. Phone books differ from place to place, so if you're not using your usual one, you may need to get familiar with different features before you can get the information you need.

How to use the telephone book

Phone books have two main divisions. First, the white pages list people's names and addresses, with each person's last name given before his or her first name or initials. The white pages also contain businesses' names and addresses, in alphabetical order. When you use the white pages, you should look up what you want by the last name of the person (say, Bochner) or the first word of the name of the business (say, Rose's if you're looking for Rose's Good Garbage). If there are a few people with the same last name as the person you are trying to look up, you should look at the first letter of the person's first name (or the initial for the first name, if that's all that appears). After you have found the right name, you will see the telephone number and address, too.

The second main division is the yellow pages, which lists businesses by the type of business they do. The types or categories are in alphabetical order. When you use the yellow pages, you look for what you need by its first letter. Look for the general category first. For instance, if you want to find a Chinese restaurant, you look under R, for "restaurants," not under C for "Chinese." Then, when you find what you need, you get specific. For example, after you find the section on Chinese restaurants under the restaurant category, you can look for the one with the location you need.

Sometimes businesses put ads in the yellow pages that tell about themselves. These ads make it easier to decide what's right for you. In fact, the phone book is a very important way of advertising any business.

There is an index in the back of the book that can help you find the things you need. So, if you are not sure how something is listed, look at the back of the yellow pages. The index lists things under different names to help you.

For example, if you want to buy tickets to the ball game, you might look up "Tickets." But nothing is listed. Look at the index under "Tickets" and you will be told to look up such categories as "Airline Ticket Agencies," "Railroads," "Steamship Agencies," "Travel Agencies," or "Ticket Sales—Entertainment and Sports." Now you can find the ticket information you want under "Ticket Sales—Entertainment and Sports" in the main part of the book.

It is very important to use the telephone book and to get used to looking things up in one. Calling Information (or Directory Assistance) instead of looking up the number yourself costs money. Even though you might need help occasionally, you can quickly learn how to find and use a phone book's details.

How to use the Internet

You can use the Internet to find the same information contained in a phone book—and more. Search engines such as 411.com, bigyellow.com, and google.com, are great resources. Every Web site is different, so it might take a while to become an expert at using each one. You should also look

at the Web sites of the companies you are interested in learning about—they contain a whole lot more information than an ad in the phone book, and they will help you understand the businesses much better. Surfing the Internet can really help you build your business. You can look for business strategies that work and for some that don't, search for folks in the same business as you and try to learn from their Web sites, find a group that gives advice to people in your business, and more—the possibilities are endless, and using the Internet is free! If you don't have a computer at home, go to your school or local library and use theirs.

As we said earlier, remember to be safe while you're using the Internet. Never sign up for anything or give out any information about you or your family without asking your parents. This is a good rule of thumb in all your business dealings.

Skill 6: Negotiating

To get what you want, you might have to give something, too.

Businesswise Bobby

Definition

Negotiation is the way you work out a contract—it's a discussion between two or more people or groups about the terms of an agreement. We talk more about contracts in chapter 13. Making deals and signing contacts are crucial steps for all businesses.

Know what you want

When you start negotiating a contract, you should always know what you want. Always ask for it clearly and directly, at the start of negotiations. For example, if you know you want to be paid $8.00 an hour to mow lawns, you should tell your prospective clients what you charge as soon as you discuss your services with them. You might get what you want without much discussion or any conflict. That sometimes happens, but not usually. Most people will not be willing to give you everything you ask for. But there are many ways you can get what you want. Do as much as you can to get it.

Listen to others

When you are negotiating a contract, you should always know what the other person wants. You need to know because if you don't, you might offer that person something he or she doesn't want. You can learn what that person wants by listening.

Find something you have that the person you are negotiating with can use

If you have a problem negotiating and nobody wants to give anything up, you can offer to give a free service or promise to refer business to the person you are negotiating with. Doing this may help move the negotiation along.

Don't be intimidated

When you are negotiating, never be intimidated by the other person, especially if he or she is an adult. That person may be just as afraid as you are. If you never get intimidated, then you are probably a good negotiator. When you negotiate, you should hold your ground. Don't easily give up what you want.

CHAPTER 13

§

Skill 7: Putting it in writing

I always get it down on paper.

Prudent Paul

After you negotiate a contract with your parents or anybody else you are doing business with, you should always put your agreement in writing. When you do that, your agreement becomes a contract you can count on. If you disagree with the person who made the contract about what it says, you can always read the contract together. If nothing is in writing, it's the other person's word against yours.

W.M.C. Contract

DATED: _____

Gail Goalsetter, from now on called **"The Waste Management Consultant"** (WMC), and Parent, from now on called "The Customer," agree as follows:

1. The WMC will prepare a Water Audit together with a report and recommendations for saving money at no initial cost to The Customer.

2. The Customer will let The WMC look at the meter, toilets, and all areas necessary for audit.

3. The Customer will follow at least the three most important recommendations in the report.

4. The WMC will prepare a monthly savings report using the bills supplied by The Customer and receive 50 percent of the savings directly from The Customer.

5. If The Customer does not do the first three important recommendations, The WMC will receive the sum of $25 for the work done in the report.

6. The audit will be completed 60 days from the signing of this Agreement.

Gail Goalsetter
Waste Management Consultant

May 5, 2007

Mrs. J. A. Jones
Parent

May 5, 2007

There are many other reasons why you should put your agreements in writing. If you don't, the other person might do something you didn't agree she should do (or not do something she said she would). Another reason is that you might lose money. If the other person is a boss and gives you less than the original bargain, you can't prove what is really owed to you. If you had a contract, you could prove it. But the main reason to have a contract is to avoid misunderstandings and to prevent fights.

What to put in a contract

There are a few things you have to include in a written contract. You must put in the names of the people who are involved. You must list the date the contract was signed. You must write down what the people involved have to do (that's the most important thing). You also have to include when the people in the contract have to do their tasks. Another very important thing to put into your contract is how much the people involved get paid, who will pay them, and when.

What to do about problems with the other person

If the other person doesn't do the agreed-on things in your contract, you can talk about the problem and show him or her the contract again. If that doesn't help, you can write a polite business letter insisting that the contract be followed. If the problem continues, you should definitely refuse to work for or do business with that person anymore.

At this point, you can (and should) tell your parents. They might help you or work with you to let others know you were treated unfairly. For example, if a local business cheated you and then wouldn't talk with you, your parents could help you tell your story to the local newspaper. Businesses don't like it when the public hears bad things about them—especially if they've cheated kids!

How to change the deal if it doesn't work

Sometimes, when things are not going well with a deal, you can find out the problem by talking things over with the other person. For example, if someone is not paying you on time to mow the lawn, he might not like your work, or he might have forgotten to pay because someone at his home might have been sick. That's why it helps to talk. You or the other person may feel that the original deal was a mistake. Many times, new deals can be worked out.

If the deal doesn't work, you can tell the other party that you don't like the way the arrangement is going, and that you want to renegotiate the deal. If you both agree, you should write the word void on the old contract and each sign your name near the word. This means the contract does not apply anymore. Then you should write up a new contract with the new terms you have agreed to.

Skill 8: Marketing & advertising

Pick a target market

A *target market* is a group of people who are just the kind of people who may want to use your product or service. To find your target market, you have to imagine who they are. For instance, if you are pet-sitting, you may want to look for people who have pets and are going on vacation.

Another way to find a target market is to do a test. Offer your service to people of different age groups, and see who buys your services. Or sell things to boys and girls, and keep track of how many of each thing they bought. Keeping records of who bought from you is the most important thing you can do to discover your target market.

Trying to sell to everyone is a lot of work. You make more money faster if you can go right to the people who want you and your product.

One way of marketing is called *direct mail*. You will read about many others later on. With direct mail, you send a letter to people and ask them to buy your product by sending in money. You can also use e-mail. This is a difficult way to market because many people see this as junk mail or e-mail spam. You might want to test the market before sending direct mail or e-mail.

Here's the story of a real test done by our mom to find the target market for her newsletter. She wanted to see if her newsletter appealed to an older or younger market, so she bought a list of names and addresses (there are companies that sell these lists, usually for about eighty dollars per thousand names). She chose one list where the people were over the age of sixty-five and one where the people were between thirty-five and fifty-five, and she then sent them both the same piece of direct mail. She knew her target market would be whichever group responded better!

When our mom did this, it gave Arthur an idea. He wanted to see if he could sell his Magic the Gathering cards directly to kids, instead of only in the store. This would give him another outlet for sales. A direct mail package from a company called ValPak came to our home. Maybe you have seen these packages or something like them. Stores and other businesses in the neighborhood pay to be included in a mailing, and they offer a discount or premium to the customer. A coupon for the offer is included in the pack.

This is an inexpensive way to advertise, but it was still too expensive for Arthur. So he asked the local pizza store owners if they would offer a free Magic the Gathering card (which Arthur would provide) to the first 100 kids who asked for it. They said yes and agreed to mention this premium in their ValPak coupon. Arthur gave them 100 cards free to give away. So, what was he hoping to get out of this?

If lots of kids asked for a card, he would know that they had read the coupons and were interested in what he had to sell. If very few people bothered to ask for the freebie, he would know kids either had not read the coupons or didn't care about Magic the Gathering. If the test was a success, Arthur would save money by later putting his own mail-order coupon in the pack.

What makes your target market want what you have to offer?

People's decisions about whom to do business with can be based on many things. Some people may like a good price and not expect the best work. Others don't mind a high price as long as the job is done very well. Still others like the job done quickly. To have a successful business, you have to be able to accommodate your best customers and give them what they want. Once you have customers, take a survey. Find out what they like about your business and keep doing it. Ask them what needs improvement and fix it. Your business will get better and better.

How will you get your target market to listen to you?

You must *market* and *advertise* your businesses. No business makes money if no one knows it's there!

What is marketing?

The way to get to the target market is by marketing. *Marketing* is everything a business does to get its target market (customers) to know about it and buy its product or service. This includes finding the target market, testing the market, and advertising.

What is advertising?

Remember, marketing includes everything from determining the right price to charge and adding to your target market, to improving your product and getting people to buy your product or use your services. One way of marketing is *advertising,* or getting across the message about your business.

There are many ways for you to advertise. One way is to pay for radio ads, although those may be too expensive for you. You can also put an ad in the newspaper. There are free ways to advertise, too. Put up signs on telephone poles (check local laws first and ask your parents about whether it's okay) and on bulletin boards in your school, your town hall, or other local places. Another way is to make *flyers,* or pieces of paper that advertise your business, and pass them out (again, make sure your parents know what you're doing). It helps if you make your flyers colorful. A third way is to make *business cards,* or cards that tell the name of your business, your business telephone number, and your name.

What is publicity?

Another popular way of marketing a business is through unpaid advertising called publicity. Instead of choosing a TV or radio station or magazine and buying ad time or space, you can get people on the station or reporters for the magazine to mention you. This is called publicity, and it works if you tell them something newsworthy, fun, or different about your company or yourself. For instance, when this book was first published, Arthur got a lot of publicity because he was very young to be an author.

You must think of something unique about your business and tell it to those with the power to tell others. You can do this by writing a press release that tells your story. Find the people who can tell the world about you by looking at the pages of newspapers for the names of editors and writers.

13-YEAR-OLD BRINGS MAGIC TO OUR TOWN

A new business has arrived in town. The business is run by Arthur Bochner. He is selling cards for a popular game that is taking the country by storm. The game is called Magic the Gathering. The manufacturer, Wizards of the Coast, did not make enough cards to meet the demands of all of the people who play the game. As a result of this, local stores have a shortage of cards. Arthur Bochner is supplying cards to anxious youngsters through the local card store on Main Street. Because of this, the people who live in the area have an ample supply of cards. Bravo!

Important points for a press release

1. Name of business

2. How to get the product

3. Where to get the product

4. Date of events (if any)

5. A catchy title

6. Something unique

7. A quote

You can go to a newspaper's Web site and get contact information for the paper and for reporters you might want to contact. Newspapers are always looking for a good story, so make sure you have something interesting to tell them!

Don't get discouraged if you don't get publicity right away. Even one mention helps your business enormously. Take it from us, stories about kids in business are in demand. Call your local radio station, even if it's a music station with no talk. If you have something interesting to say, you might get

---

Successful Sam's Healthy Lemonade Stand to Open This Weekend!

FOR IMMEDIATE RELEASE   January 15, 2007

Contact: Successful Sam

Smithtown, NY–Today, **Successful Sam** announced the opening of a **new lemonade stand** featuring fresh, healthy lemonade, plus spring water and low-fat, sugar-free cookies.

"I'm very excited to be bringing healthy, delicious treats to our neighborhood," said Sam. "I hope people will come on by and visit often."

Successful Sam's Healthy Lemonade Stand will be open at the corner of Main and Broad Streets on Saturdays and Sundays from 10:00 a.m. to 3:00 p.m., starting this weekend.

---

interviewed. We've even heard of a disc jockey who dedicated a song to the opening of a new business after its kid owner called in the request.

What is promotion?

Sometimes you can't think of anything unique about your business, and you have to create something to write a press release about. This is called *promotion*. You can give hats away to people who buy your stuff, have a clown at your lemonade stand, get a famous person to appear at an event, or give some of your profits to charity. Now you have something to say in your press release.

What are special incentives?

Sometimes you must give your customers more of an incentive to buy your product or use your services—that is, you need to offer something extra. There are many ways to go about this, and all are part of marketing.

You can give away goodies such as a pencil with your name on it, free with every purchase. This is called a *premium*. It's a business all by itself. Every year there are conventions of people in the premium business, with hundreds of booths showing Frisbees, caps, yo-yos, and other freebies.

By far, the most-used method of giving extra is the sale. *Sale* is a magic word in business; but people are suspicious of phony sales. Some companies pretend to be going out of business when they really aren't. They make you think that their stuff is very cheap because they must get rid of it before they close their doors. This is not fair, and there are laws against this type of business practice. Lying to your customers is the fastest way to go out of business.

But there are lots of good ways to handle sales—and lots of different ways to describe sales.

Of course, the two terms in the first line below mean the

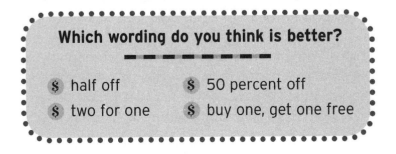

Which wording do you think is better?

$ half off $ 50 percent off

$ two for one $ buy one, get one free

same thing, so you could use either one. That's true for the two terms in the second line, too. And if you bought two of one item, all of these terms would mean you'd get the same deal! But all of these terms sound different—and get different results. You have to test your market to see which gets the best results.

Sometimes you want to make a limited-time offer or give something away for a short time only. These are legitimate ways of giving the customer an extra reason to buy what you're offering.

Two Ways to Give Your Customer a Bargain

This week only: Puppets $10.00 each— a $5.00 saving! usually $15.00

This week only: Buy a puppet for $15.00 and get $5.00 off your next purchase.

To get ideas about good ways to offer incentives, pick out newspaper, TV, or Internet advertisements that make you think, "Wow, that's a good deal!" Look at how those are worded. Ask your parents, other family members, and your friends what kinds of extras they like best when buying things they need or want. By doing this detective work, you'll get a better idea about which special touches can help your own business stand out.

What is the public relations and advertising business?

As you can see, it takes talent to think up ways to market a business. I bet you're not surprised to learn that you can sell that talent if you have it. If you do, you're a public relations agent or consultant. (In chapter 20 we give lots of information about how to be a different kind of consultant.) Many people do the job of getting businesses better known. They call the radio and TV stations, write press releases, handle promotional events, and much more.

Other people are in a related business called advertising. They are hired by companies to create and write ads, buy airtime on radio or TV, and purchase space in print and on the Internet. Many of them get creative awards for their work.

Isn't advertising difficult?

Advertising is not hard. You may think that it is harder for a kid, but it is not. You can make your posters, business cards, brochures, and flyers at home with construction paper and markers. You can also make all those things on your home computer if you have the right software.

There are a few things that are good to put in your brochures or ads. It's good to have a logo (a symbol that signifies your business) or a picture of your own face on your brochure or ad. List the three most important benefits of what you are selling. Be sure the ads let your readers know how to find you and what your goods or services cost.

We have a friend who made money by making flyers for

other kids in business. Helping other people to advertise and market their businesses might be a good business for you!

Testimonials

A *testimonial* is a statement of praise made by a person who has used your product or service. Testimonials show that you have satisfied customers. You can use testimonials in your advertising by including them in brochures, reading them on the radio, or putting them in your newspaper ads or even on your products. Can you find the testimonials in this book?

Things to Do

Call or write to the **Direct Marketing Association** (www.the-DMA.org, 1120 Avenue of the Americas, New York, NY 10036; 212-768-7277) in order to get more information about marketing and advertising.

Skill 9:
Networking

What is networking?

Networking is a way to expand a business by helping others. Having a network means that when you do something for somebody else, that person or company probably will do something for you. For example, if they know any people who could benefit from your services, they will tell those people about your business. Another thing they can do for you is give you free or discounted services or products.

How do you network?

To start networking, meet as many people as you can—people you can help and who can help you. Do favors for them. You might get something in return. Here are some other ideas.

Keep names of suppliers

When you buy a product from a certain company all the time, you should keep the company's business card so you can call them if you need help with something or if you have a problem with their product. If they do something nice for you, you should do something for them, like giving away some of your services free or charging a lower price.

Do special things for others

You can offer lower prices or free services to people who help you out. You can also refer people to the businesses that have helped you.

Be careful with networking

When picking out the people you want in your network, be sure they have products or services you can use. Also, make sure that the people and companies in your network are the kinds of people and companies who will do something for you. And, finally, make sure those folks are trustworthy. You don't want to get a bad reputation because you are friendly with or do business with people who aren't fair, honest, and reliable.

Skill 10:
Human relations

Human relations is the way people interact with one another. In business, human relations is also about figuring out what people's habits are and then later accommodating those in your practices.

Know people's needs

When you go into business, you must learn what the needs are of people in your area. This knowledge can help you choose what business you will go into. If you already have a business, this can help you in a different way: you can change your business to suit your customers' needs. If your business suits the needs of your community, you will do well. For example, if there is no pet-sitting service in your community and a lot of your neighbors go on vacation, then you might decide to start a pet-sitting business.

Know the habits of the people around you

In business, it is important to know the habits of your customers and potential customers. For instance, if your business involves going to the library to exchange books for your whole family (see Business 9, in chapter 18), this kind of knowledge is useful. If the book a particular family member wants is out, what do you do? If you know what kinds of books this person likes to read, you can pick out another book for him or her. If you don't know, you probably won't get anything for that person. That might make the person mad enough to stop using your services.

Be courteous and polite

When you talk to people in business, you have to be nice to them, as we discussed earlier. You should never be rude, even if a person is giving you a hard time. Always use good manners. When dealing with people who have complaints about your business, you should always be sensitive to their needs and try to help them as best you can.

PART 3

$

Twenty super businesses you can start right now

CHAPTER 17

Two big businesses for kids

Business 1: Lucrative Lemonade

The big picture

Lemonade? Oh no, not another lemonade stand! Yes, the old standby is back, but it's different! This lemonade stand has a modern, health-conscious spin. It sells only preservative-free, low-sugar lemonade. Only fresh lemons, distilled or filtered water, and a little bit of sugar are used. Serve carob chip cookies (instead of chocolate chip) or other healthy treats of your choice. Cookbooks will give you great ideas for all kinds of delicious home-made, good-for-you snacks.

Here's how to start this healthy business:

$ **Buy the supplies** you need to make your lemonade and other treats.

$ **Test the amount** of each ingredient to get the best taste. Create an original recipe (good for advertising), if possible. Try different amounts of everything. Taste test with your family.

$ **Set up your selling stands** at the same location at the same times each week, and advertise so people will know you are there. In front of your home or on your porch is okay, but even better is a busy location such as a safe shopping area.

Here's a twist for the lemonade! Work with a public organization or charity to share the profits, and get the use of their grounds in return. For example, outside of schools on Friday afternoons, outside of places of worship after services, and outside of libraries after they close on Saturdays are all locations that might work for you.

Once your business is up and running, you can *franchise* it, meaning you can write a contract so that your friends would pay you a certain amount to use your recipe, advertising, supplies, business name, signs, or marketing techniques. In return, they would pay you the cost of your supplies and a *flat fee* (a single agreed-on amount) to go into your lemonade business. Like Burger King and McDonald's, you can become a franchise mogul.

Here's one important area where the government protects business. You can trademark your name and copyright your recipes if they are really unique. That way, no one can use them without your permission. All it costs is a few dollars and lots of paperwork. To learn more, visit the U.S. Copyright Office's Web site (www.copyright.gov) and type "recipe" into the search field.

$$-$$$$

This business can create a lot of profit if you stick with it. Another way you can turn lemon yellow into dollar green is by using the franchise idea. That can really help you be known throughout your town. Ask your friends if they would like to have a franchise.

Kid's capital

The capital you must put up for this job is high. You will need money to buy your food supplies and recipe books, set up your stand, and advertise and market your products. You will also need to put in lots of time—time to make the lemonade and the other treats to sell, to scout out areas where you can sell your products, to make signs to advertise, and, eventually, to get your franchise going.

Franchising is a great way to make a lot of money in this business. If you get a lot of franchises, you can have a full-blown big business!

Marvin Mogul

Skills

For this business you will need to know how to test the lemonade and other treats, how to find places to sell your products, how to start a franchise, and how to keep your business going for a long time. Perhaps the most important skill that is needed is record keeping.

Your Business on the Web

If you're having trouble finding the right recipe for your lemonade, search for one on the Internet. You can use recipes you find online and change them to make them your own. Food sites such as **www.foodtv.com** and **www.epicurious.com** are great resources.

Steps to success

($) **Collect all the materials** you will need.

($) **Make test batches** of lemonade and treats, and test them with your family.

To be successful in this business you must be able to keep good records. If you keep good records, you will know if your business is making money or losing money. Record keeping is the key!

Irwin Earner

$ **Scout out places** to sell your lemonade and treats.

$ **Sell the lemonade** and treats.

$ **Set up franchises.**

Business 2: Designer Dollars

The big picture

This business is for the artistically inclined. You create sweatshirts and T-shirts with your own unique designs on them. Use cloth paint, glitter, buttons, stencils, and anything else you can think of. You should use high-quality sweatshirts and T-shirts (such as Hanes or Fruit of the Loom), especially since you can get a better price when you sell the garments.

Another idea, instead of making up your own designs, is making *personalized* shirts. That means you can put whatever the customer wants on the shirt, such as the person's name and a design.

As for where to sell your product, the possibilities are endless. You can go to county fairs, flea markets, and expos. If you want to go into stores with your product, you can do that in many ways. You might want to sell to baby stores or clothing stores, for example. You can sell on *consignment,* which means that you give a store your product to sell, and if people buy it, the store pays you. If nobody buys your product from the store, the store gives it back to you. (We also discuss consignment with Business 14, in chapter 19.) You can also sell your products to the store outright, which means that the store pays you for your goods and then doesn't give any of them back to you (nor do they give you a percentage of the money they make by selling them).

Your Business on the Web

You can easily take this business on the Internet by visiting sites that allow you to set up online store fronts. One great site that specializes in products designed by individuals is **www.cafe-press.com**. You can sign up, upload designs you've made on your computer for everything from T-shirts to mugs, and then start selling right away. You don't even have to pay! When someone buys something from your Cafe Press page, the company takes a cut. Of course, you'll have to let people know you're selling on the site, so don't forget to advertise. As usual, get permission from a parent before you do anything online.

When you buy your supplies to make your shirts, comparison shop. You will save some money that way.

Penelope Pennypincher

You can also sell *wholesale,* which means that you give a discount to a person or a store who buys a lot of one product. Another way to sell would be by working with a charity. For example, whenever a person buys a shirt, a percentage of your earnings would go to the charity. In exchange, the charity would help you advertise.

This business requires a *marketable skill,* which means a skill you can sell as part of your goods and services—in this case, fashion designing. And this fact brings us to one of the hardest parts of going into business: pricing. In this business, you have to decide how much you are going to charge for your products—and pricing can be difficult. It depends on many things. One of the major things is the quality of the shirts you use, since you can charge more if you have high-quality products. You should take into account *all* of your expenses when pricing. Also, you should always check out the competition's pricing before you price your own goods.

You might want to visit department stores to check prices of goods similar to what you want to offer. If you stencil in the designs on your shirts, you might want to charge less than the stores. If you do the designs freehand and do them well, you can charge more. To give you an idea of an appropriate price, Rose checked with a friend of hers who does this, and she charges fifteen dollars for a sweatshirt and twelve dollars for a T-shirt. The sizes are for children three to six years old. The designs are stenciled, and she personalizes the shirts.

$$$-$$$$

This business can be very profitable. If you know where to go to sell your product, and if you are a good salesperson, you will make a lot of money. Also, if your shirts look nice, you will sell a lot of them.

Kid's capital

The capital needed for this business can be very high. You will need a lot of money to buy your supplies. You can find

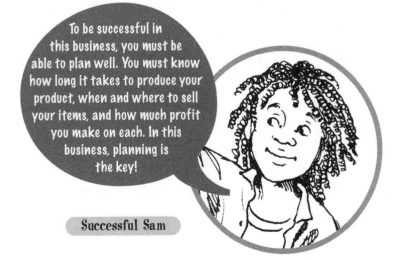

To be successful in this business, you must be able to plan well. You must know how long it takes to produce your product, when and where to sell your items, and how much profit you make on each. In this business, planning is the key!

Successful Sam

supplies online, in craft stores, and in bargain clothing stores. And you will need money to get tables at flea markets. You will also need time to get your supplies, make your shirts, and go around selling your products to stores. Of course, if you sell only online, your expenses will be much lower.

Skills

For this business you will need to have *supply savvy,* which means you must be able to find your needed supplies at the lowest possible price. You will also need to know how to paint or stencil in the designs that go on your shirts (or how to use a computer program to make them). And you will need to know how to sell your product.

Steps to success

- $ **Buy** all your supplies.

- $ **Produce** one to five sample shirts.

- $ **See which designs** you and your family like best.

- $ **Get a table at a flea market** or county fair, sell to stores, or sell on the Internet.

- $ **Keep your designs fresh** and trendy.

Seven old standbys with moneymaking twists

The businesses we describe in this chapter are ones you may already have tried or read about. They are the traditional kids' businesses. But with all the new skills you're learning, they can have lots of new moneymaking twists.

Business 3: Raking in Riches
The big picture

Leaf raking is a time-honored job for kids. It's easy, it can be fun, and it's also needed in suburbia far and wide. People who are elderly or who simply don't have enough time may need kids to perform this task for them. All that has to be done for this business is to ask potential customers if they need raking done. You can charge different amounts for different-sized yards. If you are a city kid, you'll find that some

To be successful in this business, you must know your customers. When you know your customers, you will better understand their needs.

This is one of my personal-favorite businesses. I like it because it is so easy and can make a profit.

Marvin Mogul

brownstone houses have gardens, yards, and trees in the back where you could rake.

$$-$$$$

The leaf-raking job can be very profitable. The profit will depend on how big your customers' lawns are, how often you rake, and how much you charge.

Kid's capital

The capital needed for this business is mostly time, but some money is needed, too. Money will be needed for advertising and for supplies. As far as supplies, you will need one or two rakes (rakes may break, so having an extra couldn't hurt) and plastic garbage bags for carrying the leaves. There is one more thing you may want to buy, but it's optional: a wheelbarrow. You might want to have one to carry all your supplies back and forth from your jobs. Wheelbarrows can be expensive, so buy one only if you need to.

Skills

The skills needed for this business are marketing, human relations, and negotiating.

Steps to success

 Buy rakes and garbage bags.

(\$) **Put up signs** around town.

(\$) **Visit** all new customers.

(\$) **Rake** and bag the leaves.

Business 4: Green Growth from Lawn Mowing

The big picture

The lawn-mowing business can be a pleasure to undertake, but there can be a major expense involved: a lawn mower. You probably can't afford to purchase your own lawn mower, so if you have one, you're doing great. If not, you could consider saving up for one or striking a deal with your parents. If they buy a lawn mower, you give them a percentage of your profits. Lawn mowers can also be rented, or the person whose lawn you're mowing may have one.

The actual service you provide is mowing the lawns of the people in your neighborhood. If you have a state-of-the-art mower, feature that in your advertising, since that fact will help you drum up more business. You can charge different prices for different-sized lawns. As with the leaf-raking business, your target customers will be elderly people and people who simply don't have enough time to do their own yard work.

$-$$$$

With this job you can make a huge amount of money if you already have a lawn mower and if there are lots of lawns in your neighborhood. If you do not have a lawn mower and have to rent one, don't start the business without factoring in the cost per hour of renting. You can create income for a friend by renting a mower from him or her, instead of from a company. Remember also to factor in the cost of your fuel, unless you have an electric mower. And if you have an electric one, be sure each customer has an outlet that you can use with your mower.

Kid's capital

This business requires different amounts of capital, depending on your situation. If you already have a lawn mower, all you need is the time to mow the lawns and a little bit of money to advertise and buy gas for the mower. As we've said, the capital you need is much greater if you do not have a mower, since you will need to buy or rent a mower, in addition to mowing the lawns and buying gas for the mower.

Skills

The skills needed for this business are advertising, human relations, and negotiating. A useful additional skill includes

Successful Sam

Make sure the gas you buy for your mower is environmentally safe. Strict environmentalists don't approve of power lawn mowing at all. If you are one of those, use an electric mower or a rotary, push-it-yourself mower. The push mowers can be cheaper, but they can also take more time to use. On the plus side, the fact that your mower is environmentally friendly might help you attract customers.

> To be successful in this business, dependability and consistency are the keys. Choose a time to show up, and mow each lawn regularly.
>
> **Responsible Rhoda**

telephoning: using the yellow pages or Internet to find lawn mower rental companies, and then calling to get the best price.

Steps to success

§ **Put up ads** around your neighborhood.

§ **Gather your equipment.**

§ **Negotiate a contract** with each customer.

§ **Show up on time** to mow the lawns.

Business 5: Nursery Duty

The big picture

Hey, it's a dirty job, but somebody has to do it. Nursery duty is a business in which you offer two different services to your clients. The first service is nursery cleaning: you offer to clean the nurseries of parents with young children. You should use only environmentally safe products because you are a *novelty* (rare in your field) when you use nontoxic products (plus, doing that is better for the babies). The second service is selling environmentally safe cleaning products, the same products that you use for cleaning nurseries. Your customers can use those products for the rest of the house.

$$-$$$$

This business can be a good moneymaker, and your profit depends on three factors: the price you charge for your

To be successful in this business, you must always come on time and do a complete job.

Make sure that all the products you use are environmentally safe. That might be very important to your customers.

Gail Goalsetter

services and products, the price you have to pay for the products you resell, and the types of services you provide. Each will make money individually, but cleaning and selling together would be better.

Kid's capital

This business requires a lot of capital. You will need money to place ads and to buy the products you are selling. You will also need time to do the cleaning needed by your clients.

Skills

Advertising and negotiating are two of the most important skills needed to perform this job. Also, knowing how to clean carefully and thoroughly would be good!

Steps to success

§ **Place ads** around town.

§ **Buy nontoxic, environmentally safe** cleaning products to be resold.

§ **Make a list** of each customer's needs.

§ **Negotiate a contract** with each customer.

§ **Report on time** to each customer's house for work.

Business 6: Rose's Good Garbage
The big picture

Rose's Good Garbage is really compost, which is the stuff you get when you let leaves and other organic materials get attacked by heat, so that they rot and form a rich, dark, dirt-like material. All those organic things give off nitrogen, a gas that helps plants to grow.

People who like to garden will want to buy your product because it will help them have healthy plants. They will buy your compost at a good price because it is very expensive to buy in the plant shops. This is one of the businesses we both tried when we were younger.

$$$$

Creating, bagging, and selling compost is a great way to make money because profits are high and you don't have many costs. You can sell your bags (with, say, ten pounds per bag) of compost for ten dollars each.

Kid's capital

To create the compost, you will need leaves from your garden, plus some banana peels or other organic material, such

Package compost in small, colorful bags tied with ribbon, and sell it as designer garbage for indoor-plant lovers. It could become the next craze.

Marvin Mogul

Successful Sam

To be successful, you must be able to charge the right price, and you must be able to let people know about your business through advertising. This business works best in neighborhoods where people garden but rarely make their own compost.

as apple cores or onion skins. You'll need a rake to work with the compost while it is forming, which takes weeks or sometimes months, and you'll need a place to prepare and store the compost. Once your compost is ready for use, you'll need to put it in plastic garbage bags to be sold.

Skills

The main skills you need for this business are advertising and marketing. Also, you need to be able to get the word out about your new business.

Steps to success

Ⓢ Make sure you have **enough compost** to fill your orders.

Ⓢ Keep your **compost in neat piles.**

Ⓢ **Keep your prices competitive** with those of major companies.

Ⓢ **Keep good records** of your sales and your advertising costs.

Ⓢ **Make nice packages** out of your plastic bags.

Business 7: Profits from Plants
The big picture

Outdoor and indoor plants are very expensive, but if your family is like ours, they love flowers and greenery. There are two ways you can save money on plants and even create a big business. First, don't let your family's plants die; be in charge of watering, pruning, and feeding. Second, learn how to take cuttings from plants, root them, and grow them into large, healthy plants. If you do this well enough at home, you can even start a home-based plant-sale business right in your own front yard.

$$$$

If you know how to market, this can be a big business. Every plant you own is a little manufacturer of new plants you can sell.

Kid's capital

Time and some money are needed for this business. You need to buy rooting material and pots.

Skills

The most important skill you will need is business budgeting. You will need to find and use wholesale suppliers to keep your costs down, and you will need to find a good place to sell your plants.

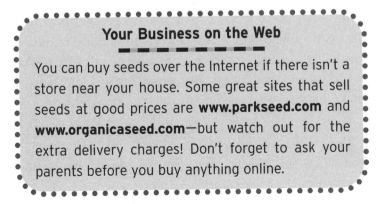

Your Business on the Web

You can buy seeds over the Internet if there isn't a store near your house. Some great sites that sell seeds at good prices are **www.parkseed.com** and **www.organicaseed.com**—but watch out for the extra delivery charges! Don't forget to ask your parents before you buy anything online.

To be successful in this business you must be able to keep good records of how much you make and how much you spend.

Steps to success

§ **Use the library** to find books on growing plants from cuttings.

§ **Experiment** until you have some inventory.

§ **Market your product** to your family first if they are frequent plant buyers.

§ **Market to the public.**

§ **Keep excellent business records.**

Business 8: Great Gains from Garage Sales
The big picture

There are many ways to do a garage sale. The most efficient is by going through your own house and picking out the things you don't need or want anymore or that you've outgrown. Sell these things in your yard, at a flea market, or on the Internet—but check with your parents first!

$

The garage sale is a good way to get rid of all your stuff. However, when you sell your products, you will receive less than you originally paid for them.

Your Business on the Web

We don't know who made up the name, but selling old things you don't need around the house is called having a **garage sale.** But to have a garage sale, you don't need to have a garage! You can sell at online auction sites like **eBay.com** or online stores like **Amazon.com.** Ask your parents to help you set up an account, and start selling! You only pay the sites money if your item sells, so you don't need any money to get started. Of course, you'll have to ship your items, but the buyer should pay for the shipping (each site has different rules, so check them out before you sign up).

Kid's capital

The things that you should sell at a garage sale (or on eBay or Amazon.com) are things you already have. Most of those things will be games, toys, and the like. The biggest capital you risk in a garage sale is your time. Paid advertising is good for garage sales, so you may want to make an advertising budget as well. If you don't sell enough things, however, you might lose money.

Skills

The skill you need most in a garage sale is marketing—getting people to come to your sale. Put up signs, put ads on bulletin boards, and even put ads in the newspaper. Marketing is also selling at the right price and making the display look nice. You'll also need Web skills if you decide to sell online. As we've said before, don't forget to tell your parents what you're doing.

To be successful in the garage sale field, you must have a good attitude toward your customers. When customers are at your sale or when you deal with them online, treat them with respect.

Steps to success

$ **Make sure your prices** are clearly marked.

$ **Give a short history of each product** on the tag if it's interesting or funny.

$ **Ask your parents** if your pricing is fair.

$ **Check the weather report** (if you're not selling online), and set a date.

$ **Advertise** well in advance of the sale.

⑤ **If you're selling online,** make sure that you have an account at a reputable site and that you understand its rules. Ask your parents for help when dealing with customers!

Don't forget this date!
When: June 21, 10:00 am.
Where: 40 Central Street
What: The Best Garage Sale of the Summer
Toys, books & much more!
Free Lemonade

Business 9: Big Bucks from Books
The big picture

This project is for the family who likes to read and buys lots of books, newspapers, and magazines. Here's how to help save money: If you have a lot of books that you have already read, have outgrown, or no longer enjoy, you can trade them in for other books at a book-barter store. The books will probably be used ones, but you will probably find some you have never read.

With newspapers and magazines, you can also compare the cost of subscription buying with the price of purchasing single copies. If you find that your family buys the same magazine every month from the newsstand, see if purchasing a subscription would save money. And as suggested earlier, you can set up a library delivery service for your family. You

To be successful in this business, you must be able to be on time with your pickups, deliveries, and package shipments (if you sell online).

Responsible Rhoda

can take their book orders and go to the library once a week to fulfill them, then return those books they have finished.

$-$$$

These book-related businesses can be big money savers if you have a lot of old books or if you go to the library often and on a schedule.

Kid's capital

The only capital you need for these businesses is time. You will need time to go back and forth to the library, to take orders for books from your family, and to get books from your house to trade in for other books or sell.

Skills

The most important skill needed is human relations: how you talk to people. You need to talk to people in this project because you need to find out what they want from the library (or what magazines they like). If you can learn your family's tastes, you can continually supply them with books they want even if they don't give you specifics. You'll also need to know how to price your books and deal with customers if you decide to sell online.

The library also has CDs, videos, records, and 16-millimeter films available free.

Penelope Pennypincher

Steps to success

⑤ Gather your family's old or **used books.**

⑤ Take the books to a **book exchange** and get other books, or put your family's books up for sale on the Internet.

⑤ **Take orders from family** members for books you can pick up or return to the library.

⑤ Make sure that you **deliver the books to the library** on time.

Your Business on the Web

You can also sell your family's used books online at **Amazon.com** and other similar sites. You might get more than you would if you sold them to a local store, but you have to work a little harder. Arthur sold his used college textbooks when he graduated, and he got a lot of money back.

CHAPTER 19
$
A nifty idea

This book started with a nifty idea: that every parent or family does things that waste money in some way—usually, in lots of ways. We kids can offer to help stop the waste, provided we get a share in the money we help to save.

There's really no need to throw away clothes you can sell, pay full price for food when there are coupons, or be over-charged on your telephone bill. Still, families do these things. Why? Because parents often have no time to save money. They waste money to save time, and then they get into bad habits. Let's save money for our folks by taking the time they won't take to stop waste in the home!

Since we believe that money is right around the corner if you look for it, we started to look at home. Ever since Arthur and our mom wrote *The Totally Awesome Money Book for Kids (and Their Parents)*, Arthur has been on TV talking about money. He is always asked, "How much do you get for an allowance?" The fact is, neither of us ever got an allowance. We learned about saving in little ways. For example, even when we were very young, we started taking and saving the change that our father would leave on the dresser every night (Rose took over for Arthur when he started high school). Our dad has always known what we were doing, and he didn't mind because it was only small change. As with that change, parents might not feel that doing small things to save money around the house matters—and that's where you come in!

Parental alert:
The annoyance factor

These next few businesses are designed to make money by stopping waste in the home. A lot of the stuff you need to do to stop waste requires cooperation from your parents or a change of habits or both. You can get pretty annoying if you keep nagging your parents about being wasteful. Think about how you feel when they nag you about things.

To prevent annoyance, make sure your folks understand what you are trying to do, and have a signed contract for these home businesses that lists their duties as well as yours. You'll find a sample contract on page 83. You won't make money without your parents' approval, so keep them as partners in all you do.

Business 10: Cooking for Cash
The big picture

A big part of every family's budget is food. So cooking instead of eating out and growing your own vegetables instead of buying them are ways to save money. But they don't save time. A good way to save money is to find out your family's eating habits. Do your parents eat lunch out

CHAPTER 19

To be successful in this business, you must be able to keep records, convince your parents about the value of what you're doing, and most important, make sure your family is happy with their food.

Gail Goalsetter

when they go to work, or do they take a bag lunch? How many times a week does your family eat dinner at home?

If your family eats dinner out most nights, you might want to ask your parents if you can eat in more. (This may be even easier to do if you try the ideas in Business 18, which we discuss in chapter 20.) If your family eats in a lot, try growing your own fruits and vegetables.

After you have convinced your parents to eat in more often, you can take the next step in saving money with food. You offer your parents your services as a shopper, and as with the earlier consulting businesses, you take a cut (percentage) of the money your family saves. For instance, instead of buying one package of rice every time your family goes shopping, you can buy the rice *in bulk*, which means buying a lot of one product at the same time. For example, buying a ten-pound bag of rice at four dollars is cheaper than buying ten boxes of rice at sixty cents a pound.

$$$$

This project can be a big moneymaker for you as a consultant if you stick to it.

Kid's capital

The capital needed here is time. You have to give your time to go shopping with your family, to convince your parents to buy in bulk, to convince them to eat at home more, and of course to cook the meals. If you grow your own fruits and vegetables, you will need space to build your garden and money to buy seeds and fertilizer (read more about gardening in Business 7, chapter 18).

Skills

The main skills you will need here are record keeping and cooking. If you keep good records of how much you saved by eating in, growing your own fruits and vegetables, and buying in bulk, your parents will keep doing these things.

Steps to success

(§) Find out whether your **family eats in or out** the most.

(§) **Convince your parents** to eat in more often.

(§) Try to **grow your own** fruits and vegetables.

(§) Go shopping with your family and **buy products in bulk.**

(§) Keep good records so that your family will see that they are saving money.

Business 11: Extra Capital from Couponing

The big picture

Coupons are a way of giving shoppers a bargain so they will buy a product. The coupons are given by the manufacturers of the products. Coupons give you money off the price

Shopping List

Item	Coupon File	Amount Saved	Brand
Juice	File J(uice)	$.20	Tropicana
Spaghetti sauce	File S(auce)	2 for 1	Ragu
Cereal	no coupons	—	—
Milk	File D(airy)	Free cream with gallon of milk	Borden

at the cash register, let you buy two for the price of one, or send you back a gift or money in the mail *(a rebate)*.

Good shoppers use coupons for the things they want in the first place, not to buy stuff they don't need just because they get money off. But it takes time to find, cut out, and organize coupons. That's why lots of families don't use coupons. That's where you come in—as a "couponer for profit." You can find coupons in the mail, in newspapers and magazines, and even in the stores that offer the coupons.

As with the last business, you should work to find the cheapest products available. This may mean joining a whole-sale warehouse club such as Costco or Sam's Club. These places have some of the cheapest food around, but you have to buy in bulk. If you have a family of four, though, the amount might be perfect! To see if those clubs are right for you, list your family's favorite items and see how much they cost at one of the clubs and at your local supermarket. Which is more? Can you help your family save by changing where they shop for food?

Even if you don't have a wholesale club near you, comparison shop at all of your local supermarkets. You might find one is cheaper than the rest—and beware of supermarkets that are normally high-priced but give you a card that will help you save. Often, the lower, card-member price is about the same as at a regularly priced market.

$$

Couponing can be labor intensive, but you can save a lot of money by doing this.

Kid's capital

What you need for this business is *lots* of time! You'll also need a little money for magazines and newspapers if your family doesn't already get them, since that's where you may find the coupons. This business doesn't cost much to start, and your family can begin saving money immediately.

Expiration Date Alert

Orange juice: two-for-one,   expires March 3

Garbage bags: 25 cents off,   expires April 6

Spaghetti sauce: 30 cents off,

today is the last day

Skills

The main skill in this business is organization, especially with record keeping and filing. A coupon-filing system that shows the expiration dates (after which you can't use the coupons) and a checklist for the shopper are essential for this project.

You may have to spend a lot of time on this project, but it will be well worth the effort because of the money you can save.

Pablo Payment

Steps to success

§ **Make a filing system** based on the foods your family buys the most.

§ **Clip coupons** wherever you see them, and place them in order, by food types.

§ Check your local **supermarket's Web site** for online deals.

§ Within each food category, **file by date,** with the expiring coupons up first.

§ Make a **weekly list** for the shopper in the family.

§ **Keep track** of what you save.

A special note from Rose

When I did research for this book, I found loads of materials on couponing. There are even couponing clubs and

Your Business on the Web

You can save money by looking for food deals online. **Amazon.com** has a food section, and your local supermarket probably has a Web site with coupons you can print and take to the store.

newsletters. If you and your family start to save good money on coupons, look at the bibliography of this book to see how to make it a real family hobby.

Business 12:
Riches through Refunding
The big picture

A *refund* or *rebate* is money you get back when you buy something. The folks who send you the money are usually the manufacturers (the ones who make what you bought). Why do they do it? Sometimes to get you to buy a new product; sometimes to find out who their customers are.

To get your refund, you must fill out a form and also send back a *proof of purchase,* something to show that you really bought the product (for example, the barcode from a carton of toothpaste or a cap from a bottle). The manufacturer will let you know what you need to send in through ads in the paper, signs in the grocery or drugstore, or coupons in the mail.

Successful Sam

Don't let your parents buy something just because it has a rebate. Otherwise, they are wasting money. Make sure the product your family buys to get your refund is something the family uses. Refunds are easiest to find for soap, paper products, toothpaste, and candy. Yum!

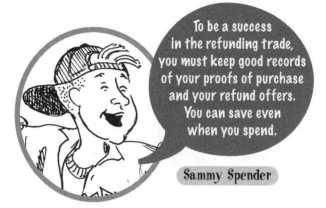

To be a success in the refunding trade, you must keep good records of your proofs of purchase and your refund offers. You can save even when you spend.

Sammy Spender

You'd be surprised how many people don't do the work to get their rebates. That's why so many companies give them out—they know only a small percentage of those folks who could get a rebate actually do what they have to do to get it. You can make money by doing all the work needed to get the rebates your parents are due. For example, your folks might not think it's worth the time to fill out a form and mail it in if they'll get only a five-dollar rebate. But *you* might. You can do the work of getting the rebates, and then ask your parents for a percentage of that amount.

$$

Refunding can make you hundreds of dollars in a year. Average refunds are one or two dollars per item, and they can amount to twenty dollars at a time if you purchase a lot of a product.

Kid's capital

You'll need a stamp and an envelope for each refund, as well as the time to look through the newspapers and coupon sources for information on refunds.

Skills

The main skills you will need are filing and organization.

The big money in refunds comes from buying only what you use anyway, not buying a product just for the refund. So it's best to save proofs of purchase in a well-organized file and use them when you can get a refund.

Steps to success

$ **Make three files:** a bag for bottles, a paper file for receipts, and a box for odd-shaped stuff.

$ **Help the family shopper unpack,** and go with him or her to the store as often as you can.

$ **Save labels,** proof-of-purchase seals, and Universal Product Code seals. (Fill and soak bottles with hot water to get the labels off.)

$ **Make a list** of the weight, size, and manufacturer of the product.

$ Keep a lookout for **refund forms** in packages, in stores, and in newspapers.

$ Ask for more mail! Visit the Direct Marketing Association's yellow pages on its Web site (**www.the-DMA.org**), and **search the Internet for coupons.** Remember to ask your parents before you give out your address or other information!

$ Ask your family shopper to **keep all cash register receipts.** You may need them, too.

$ **Keep a list of refund offers** and the dates they expire. Give the family shopper a copy of this list.

Business 13: Recycled Wealth
The big picture

Those people interested in preserving our environment do many things to help, such as recycling containers, aluminum, and many other things. Did you know that some recycling centers will pay you to receive certain types of packaging?

Check your town's or city's Web site to find out whether the dump or the recycling center will pay for certain kinds of recyclable trash. You can take your family's recycling (and eventually your neighbors' if they will let you) to the local recycling center, and take a cut of what the recycling is worth. Even if your town won't pay for recyclable trash, neighboring towns might, so don't forget to check them out as well.

To be successful in this business, you must be able to keep yourself on schedule with the pickups and drop-offs of your recyclable goods. Make a deal with your parents or your older brother or sister—if you have one—to help you make deliveries. Give them a cut of the profits.

Paul & Paula

I like the idea of making money and helping our planet at the same time.

Candy Creditworthy

The best moneymakers are

$ **aluminum,** including soda and tuna fish cans, pie plates, aluminum siding, and window frames

$ green and clear **glass** from jars, bottles, and drinking glasses

$ **newspapers,** clean and wrapped in bundles, each weighing one or two pounds

$$

This can be pure profit if your family uses lots of these materials and you're also a good hunter. However, you will never get as much as you or your parents actually paid for the recyclable goods.

Kid's capital

Very little is needed in this business except time and storage space. This is a good moneymaker for kids with garages, sheds, or covered patios. Once a month, you'll need a grownup's help in getting everything to the recycling center.

Skills

The most important skill you will need is networking. In this business the real money is made by putting out the word that you will accept clean recyclable materials from friends and neighbors.

Steps to success

$ **Call a few nearby recycling centers** and find out what they pay for glass, aluminum, and paper recyclables.

$ **Ask their requirements** for accepting goods.

$ **Find out their hours** of operation.

$ **Ask whether they will pick up** at your home or whether you must take the goods to the center.

$ **Get permission** from your parents to store the materials.

$ **Tell others** you are interested in recycling their stuff.

$ **Offer a free pickup** or offer a discount if they bring the stuff to you.

$ **Call the fire department** to find out their rules about accumulating clean trash.

$ **Separate glass from cans,** and so on.

$ **Use a magnet** to test whether a metal is aluminum (it won't attract).

Business 14: Fashionable Fortunes
The big picture

A fashionable trend today is to buy used (sometimes called slightly hurt or gently worn) clothes from resale shops. Kids' clothes sell especially well. Children grow so fast, and sometimes it doesn't pay to buy new clothes for them. Even purses, shoes, and hats are in demand. Brand-new items gotten as gifts or bought in the wrong size can be sold for almost full price.

Resale shops accept your clothes on consignment. As we

Find out if the shop also accepts used toys and books. Most do. There's lots of extra money in used games and puzzles, so try not to lose the pieces to games when you play with them.

Marvin Mogul

mentioned earlier, that means you leave your stuff with the shop, and they assign you a number and then tag your clothes with that number. If some people buy your items, the shop owners keep a running record of your account and send you a check every month or so for the purchases, depending on the shop's policy.

$

You receive one-third to one-half of the sale price of the clothes left on consignment. This business is rated low profit only because you will always receive less than your folks originally paid for your clothes. But, of course, you would get nothing if the clothes were thrown out or simply left in your drawer.

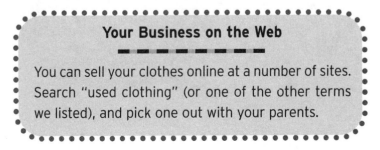

Your Business on the Web

You can sell your clothes online at a number of sites. Search "used clothing" (or one of the other terms we listed), and pick one out with your parents.

Kid's capital

You'll need the clothes themselves, a few phone calls, and the time or money to clean the garments before you take them to a shop.

Skills

The key to making money with this business is record keeping. You must know what you took to the shop (or offered online), what was sold, and how much money you received for each item. Eventually, you can test several stores to decide which are the moneymaking winners, so don't forget to keep good records.

Steps to success

$ **Look in the phone directory** under "Used Clothing," "Thrift Shops," "Recycled Clothes," "Resale Shops," and "Children's Clothing," or search the Internet for companies that deal with those things.

Instead of reselling, donate the items to charity and help your folks get a tax deduction that will save them money. Then, ask your parents for some of the money they saved. After all, they wouldn't have saved it without you!

Charitable Charlie

Collect the stuff that sells best, like baby clothes and baby toys. Ask your aunts, uncles, cousins, and other relatives if they have any extras. Offer them 10 percent of the profits.

Penelope Pennypincher

§ **Call the shop** and ask about several things: What condition must items be in? What percentage of the sale price do I get? How long do you keep items if they are not sold? Do you return items to me? What if I change my mind and want an item back? Are you part of a charity?

§ **Make a list** of all the items you want to resell. Ask your family to add to the list.

§ **Get your parents' approval** for everything on the list.

§ **Deliver the bundle** to the shop of your choice, and get them to sign the list so you both agree on what's yours.

§ Get your **consignment number** and keep a record of it.

§ If you haven't done well in a month, try a new place. Or if you have a lot of stuff, **test two places** at a time.

CHAPTER 20

$

How to set up a home waste management consulting business

Call yourself a consultant

Waste management is a special kind of business, and it takes a special kind of entrepreneur called a *consultant* (which we mentioned in chapter 14). The word *consultant* comes from the word *consult*, and it means to give advice. So you, as a home waste management consultant, must give advice on saving money by cutting down waste in your home. All entrepreneurs, no matter what business they are in, make their money selling something valuable to someone who needs it. Shop owners sell stuff; lawyers sell legal services; gardeners sell their know-how in making things grow.

As a home waste management consultant, you are selling something, too: your good ideas on how to cut costs or how to make money by stopping waste. You can make money by helping others save money—and helping the environment at the same time.

Here's what your business card might look like:

JEFFREY JONES, W.M.C.
Waste Management Consultant

(817) 555-1208

15 Maplewood Lane

Fort Worth, TX 76106

Get your valuable ideas on paper

Everybody has good ideas, but not everybody can sell them. To get money for your ideas, you have to put them down on paper so people can read them, understand them, and appreciate them. If they can't do all three, they won't give you business. Consultants can do this in a fun way that doesn't take a writing genius: an *audit and report*. Because we are home waste management consultants, we will talk about the *waste management audit and report*.

An audit is a survey, or a regularly occurring look around, to see if anything is wrong or can be improved in a particular place (usually a home or business). With a written audit, your customer will understand the problem.

For example, your audit might check for water-wasting leaks or for loose doors and windows that waste home heating fuel. Here's an example of an audit for water waste:

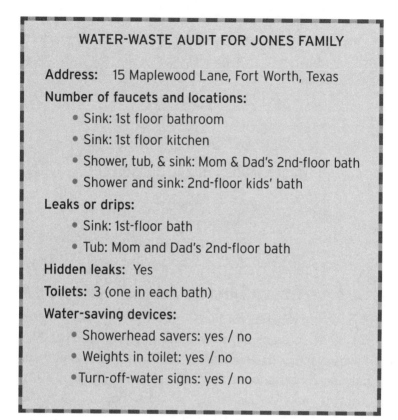

WATER-WASTE AUDIT FOR JONES FAMILY

Address: 15 Maplewood Lane, Fort Worth, Texas

Number of faucets and locations:

- Sink: 1st floor bathroom
- Sink: 1st floor kitchen
- Shower, tub, & sink: Mom & Dad's 2nd-floor bath
- Shower and sink: 2nd-floor kids' bath

Leaks or drips:

- Sink: 1st-floor bath
- Tub: Mom and Dad's 2nd-floor bath

Hidden leaks: Yes

Toilets: 3 (one in each bath)

Water-saving devices:

- Showerhead savers: yes / no
- Weights in toilet: yes / no
- Turn-off-water signs: yes / no

Just knowing what is wrong is not enough to make you a consultant. You also must know how to solve the problem. You put your ideas in a report that tells your customer how to fix what's wrong, how much the problems will cost to fix, who can fix the problems for them, and even how much they can save by carrying out the fixes.

With a report, your customers will appreciate what they need to do and how you are helping them. Here's what a report looks like:

REPORT

There are two leaks I can see in the first-floor bathroom and second-floor tub. Also, there are no water-saving showerheads and no weights in the toilet tanks.

RECOMMENDATIONS

1. Fix two faucets	Cost: $100.00	Sam the Plumber 673-2000
2. Replace two showerheads	Cost: $34.00	Linda's Hardware 736 Main Street Open 9-5, till 9 on Thurs.
3. Put plastic container filled with rocks in each toilet tank	Cost: zero	I will do it.

Estimated savings: $30.00 per month
Average water bill in the past six months: $150.00

As a consultant, you can do just the audit and report, or you can also be the one who fixes the problems you find. It depends on what skills you have and on what the problem is. Later, in our description of Business 17, we talk a lot more about ways to keep records on water waste in homes, plus ways to take care of the problems.

For example, let's say you find out that the family flushes the toilet lots of times a day and that putting a plastic jar filled with rocks in the tank can save two gallons of water with every flush. Well, preparing and placing the rock-filled jars are easy things you can do yourself. But let's say you find out that the faucet leaks and needs a new washer. Maybe you can fix it; maybe you need a plumber. In your report, you would include the name of a suggested plumber and the estimated cost.

And that point leads us to the next part of the consulting business: getting paid.

Ways consultants get paid

As a consultant, you can be paid in four different ways, depending on how you want to run your business.

1. By the hour: You have to put a price on your time, just the way you would do if you were baby-sitting. This is called an hourly rate. Let's say you want two dollars an hour. For a baby-sitter, it's easy because the parents just tell you how many hours they want, and you multiply the hours by two dollars and get paid.

5 hours of baby-sitting at $2.00 an hour:
5 x $2.00 = $10.00

A consultant does the same thing, except that he or she sets the amount of time spent. You have to know how long it will take to do the waste management audit and report. You won't really know how much time it will take until you have done a lot of them, so we don't recommend this way of getting paid for a beginner. Most beginners charge too little because they think things will go faster than they do.

2. By the audit: Give one price that you think is fair for the type of work involved—a fee. This is the way you

If you want to charge by the hour or by the job, ask others in your business what they charge.

Marvin Mogul

might charge to shovel snow or mow a lawn: you look at the size of the yard, you know what others are charging, and you give a price.

Again, beginning consultants can't do this because they don't have enough experience to get to the right price.

3. By a percentage: Bingo! This is the one for us. Let's say you do the water audit, and it saves the family fifty dollars. You get part of that savings. As we mentioned in chapter 6, this percentage is sometimes called a cut. In this way, you don't need to set a price on your time or the job.

Even more important, it's easy to get hired because the customer doesn't pay you anything unless you save or make money for them. Be sure to estimate savings in your report: multiply gallons of water by the cost per gallon to figure out how much your customers might save. This information is good for you and your customers to know.

4. Don't forget to charge for extra work: In addition to the fee, hourly rate, or cut you get for the audit and report, you must charge money for any extra work you do to solve the problem, like doing a plumbing repair or fixing a window.

If you charge a fee or an hourly rate, you just set a separate price for added work and put it on the bill. A bill is called an invoice. Here's what a consultant's invoice looks like:

INVOICE

From: Penelope Pennypincher   **Date:** July 14, 2007
To: The Pennypincher Family

- -

Work performed: Waste Management Audit and Report
Time spent: Three hours, July 10, 2007

         Hourly rate: $5.00
         Balance due: $15.00
         Fixing faucet: $10.00
         Total balance due: $25.00

If you get paid with a cut of savings or earnings, you get paid for doing these extras by taking a bigger cut. The more you do over and above the audit and report, the bigger your cut must be. For example:

INVOICE

From: Penelope Pennypincher   **Date:** July 14, 2007
To: The Pennypincher Family

- -

Work performed: Waste Management Audit and Report
Amount saved from July 10 to August 10: $50.00

         Percent due: 50% = $25.00
         Fixing faucet: $10.00
         Total balance due: $35.00

Note that you made more money with a percentage. But remember two important things: First, you have to be sure the family actually saves money, or you get nothing. Second, you have to wait to get paid until you know how much they saved. Again, you can estimate, but your estimate may not turn out to be the final figure. Getting paid with a percentage of money saved is a risk for both you and the customer. Would you prefer to know how much you're getting by getting paid by the hour, even though you might make less (or more)? It's up to you.

Know what it costs to start the business and keep it going

Every business needs time or money or both to get started and to keep going. As we said in chapter 8, this is called *capital.* For grown-ups, capital is almost always money. For us, capital is mostly our time. But some of the jobs in this book require money, too, especially for advertising and supplies.

Businesses that take little capital have *low start-up costs,* and those that take a lot of capital have *high start-up costs*. Businesses that require large amounts of your time are *labor intensive*. Ones that take little time or capital are called *cost-effective*. Fill in this chart for some of the jobs in this book:

149

Job	Capital: high/low	Type of capital: time/money	Amount of labor: high/low
1.			
2.			
3.			
4.			
5.			
6.			
7.			
8.			
9.			
10.			
11.			
12.			

Make a deal with your customer to do the work

Before you start work as a consultant, you must have a deal with your customer. The deal is an agreement between you and your customer about

$ **what** the work is

$ **when** the work will be finished

$ **how much** you will be paid

$ **when** you will be paid

$ **what happens** if you don't do the job

§ **what you expect** of the customer as far as following your recommendations

Deals can also include other things, depending on the work involved.

To make the deal fair for everyone, you need to be a good negotiator. Negotiating is an important business skill that you learned about in chapter 12.

After you make the deal, you must put it in writing—that is, you must write a contract. You'll find an example on page 83.

All these things are important to running a successful business. On the following pages, you will learn about the many consulting jobs and businesses in which you will have to use some, if not all, of the things you have just learned. And as often as you need to, look back at what you have read already.

Making money by becoming a waste detective

In this chapter we show you five different ways you can find and get rid of waste in the home, and each one will save your family and other customers money. Here's where a notebook comes in handy.

Take a family stop-waste survey. Ask your parents and older siblings where they think the family can save the most money (the phone bill, the water bill, electric bill, etc.).

Spark their imagination by reviewing the waste-saving business with them. Doing this will give them ideas about which jobs and activities will do them the most good, such as telephone surveys, water surveys, or electricity surveys.

Business 15: Treasures from Telephone Audits
The big picture

Not too long ago, there wasn't much you could do to save money on telephone bills except talk less. Today, lots of competition exists, and many telephone companies are out to win your business.

To act as a telephone consultant, you can compare the costs of different companies, go over your family's monthly bill to make sure there are no mistakes, and break down the bill by type of call to see if money can be saved by using letters, postcards, e-mails, or faxes instead. You can also do this for your family's cell phone, cable, and Internet bills (if you have any). Again, you can take a cut of savings or get paid a flat fee.

$$$

Lots of people call our mom "the Touch-Tone Kid." So, at least in our family, we were able to save a lot with a telephone audit. Your family might be the same, or it might be different.

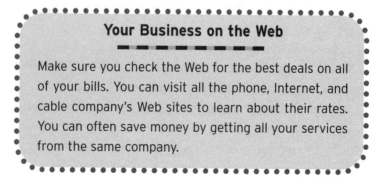

Your Business on the Web

Make sure you check the Web for the best deals on all of your bills. You can visit all the phone, Internet, and cable company's Web sites to learn about their rates. You can often save money by getting all your services from the same company.

Kid's capital

After you have done a telephone audit once, it will only take a few minutes a month to check on progress.

Skills

The most important skills you will need are research and organization. You need to be able to figure out which company will give you the best deal. You also need phone skills to help you get things straightened out with a company if the bill is wrong.

Steps to success

$ Learn to read the **phone, cable, and Internet bills.**

$ **Look at how much you pay** for renting your cable boxes and other equipment.

$ **Call various telephone companies** to get their long-distance, cable, and Internet rates (or visit their Web sites). Each company has many different plans.

$ **Look at the bills** to see which plan fits the way your family makes calls or uses the Internet.

$ **Give your family members a report** to see if they want to change the companies they use.

$ Get an **800-number telephone directory;** 800-number calls are free and can save you money.

$ Give each person a **list of the numbers** he or she uses most. This way your family members won't be tempted to use Directory Assistance to find the numbers when they're in a hurry. Every use of this service costs money.

$ **Check the bill** every month for addition mistakes, calls the family didn't make, and things that just look wrong, like a very long call or one to a place where you have no relatives or friends.

$ **Share your findings** with your family. If they confirm a mistake, you can help take care of it with the company.

Business 16: Hefty Earnings from Home Office Audits

The big picture

Your parents have a home office, though they may not think of it that way. Every family has a place where they write their checks, pile up mail, and do other work. Often it's the kitchen table. Some of your parents may have a separate room, a computer, or even a real secretary who comes to the house.

So where's the money in this for you? As with other activities, there's a lot of waste that goes along with a home office. Depending on how much work your parents do at home, you may be able to make good money as a home office auditor by getting paid a part of the amount you help your parents save.

The money you earn from this work depends on how good you are at spotting waste, finding solutions, and making the solutions work. It also depends on how much work your parents actually do at home.

Kid's capital

Time is the only capital you must have. To check online for the best deals in office supplies, you will need access to a computer. If your family doesn't have one, you can use one at your school or local library. Remember that consultants mainly spend their time, which is very valuable capital.

Skills

Research is the main skill you will need. As a consultant, you need to find better ways of doing things, better places to buy things, and things that are being done but that don't have to be done at all. All this takes knowing how to find solutions for problems. For example, if your mom or dad spends a lot of money on stamps, maybe bulk mail is the solution. You'll have to visit the post office to find out all the ways that mail can be sent cheaper than first class—that's research.

Here's a sample home office audit:

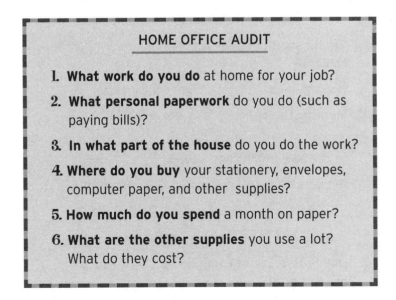

HOME OFFICE AUDIT

1. **What work do you do** at home for your job?

2. **What personal paperwork** do you do (such as paying bills)?

3. **In what part of the house** do you do the work?

4. **Where do you buy** your stationery, envelopes, computer paper, and other supplies?

5. **How much do you spend** a month on paper?

6. **What are the other supplies** you use a lot? What do they cost?

These phone audits can save you a lot of money, and your parents might let you talk on the phone more. Don't forget to do separate telephone and utility audits.

Successful Sam

Steps to success

§ **Look around** the office area, and **take notes** on things that you notice are wasteful.

§ Have your folks fill out the **home office audit sheet,** and add any questions that are important to you.

§ **Research the solutions** to their office-waste problems.

§ Check online for the **best deals on supplies.**

§ Create a **list of suggestions** on how your parents can save.

§ **Have a meeting** to tell them your ideas.

§ **Monitor the changes** they are willing to make.

§ After a month, have them fill out the audit form again to see **how much they saved.**

§ Get your share of the savings **(a consultant's fee).**

A few saving hints for the home office

§ **Use both sides of computer paper** if you are printing drafts.

§ **Sell used paper** to a recycler (see Business 13).

§ **Buy checks through the mail** instead of from the bank.

§ **Buy office furniture at thrift shops.** Make pen-and-pencil holders from painted jars.

§ **Use the Web to find deals** on everything from checks to pencils.

Business 17: Wealth in Waste-Water Audits
The big picture

A "water-works" business is a fun way to help save the environment while also saving some money. As we discussed earlier in this chapter, water costs money, so having leaks in your water system can be costly to your family and to the environment. Because we believe so much in this business, we wanted to talk more about how to make it work for you and your family.

To help save the environment and money, go around your house and look for leaks. Some common problem places are faucets, showerheads, garden hose hookups, and toilets. Did you know that 20 percent of the toilets in people's homes are leaking right now?

Here's a good way to check for leaks—ones you can see, plus some you can't. Ask your parents or any other adult in your house to show you how to read the water meter. Sometime, just before your whole family will be away from the house, check the meter and write down the number. Make sure nobody is in the house. When you come back, check the meter again. If the number is different from what it was when you left, you probably have a leak.

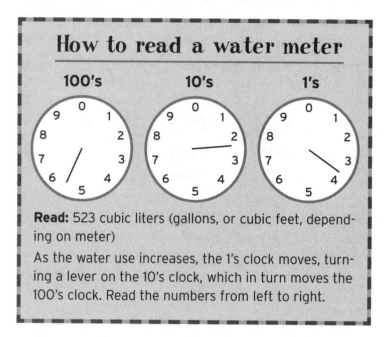

How to read a water meter

100's **10's** **1's**

Read: 523 cubic liters (gallons, or cubic feet, depending on meter)

As the water use increases, the 1's clock moves, turning a lever on the 10's clock, which in turn moves the 100's clock. Read the numbers from left to right.

It's true. Be especially careful to look for leaks in the toilet bowl. (By the way, did you know that the freshest drinking water in your house is in the toilet tank before you use it?) Now even without leaks, a toilet bowl can use more than seven gallons of water every time you flush! There are lots of ways to save some of that water.

To save water when flushing the toilet, put a one- or two-gallon bottle (say, an empty plastic one from milk or dishwashing fluid) in the back of the tank, with rocks in the bottom of it to keep it stationary. You will save one to two gallons of water every time you flush, and the toilet will work just as well. You can also talk to your parents about buying low-pressure toilets and showerheads.

$$

You can save a lot of money when you find leaks. You also have to take care of them and make sure they get fixed—and stay fixed!

Kid's capital

This is a cost-effective business, which means you can make a good profit with very little capital.. Again, as a consultant, the only capital you put up is your time.

Skills

Record keeping is the main skill you need, since you have to show your parents that you are saving them money. You also need record keeping because you need to remember where your leaks are so that you can get them fixed. And, of course, you need to be a little bit of a detective! The ideas we discussed earlier in this chapter about water-waste record keeping and reporting should help you build this into a great business.

Steps to success

$ Make sure you know how to **read the water meter.**

$ Check around the house for any **type of leak.**

$ **Tell your parents** about the leaks.

$ Get the **leaks fixed.**

$ Recommend other **water-saving measures** (new toilets, showerheads, and so on).

Business 18: Revenues from Restaurant Audits

The big picture

If your family eats out a lot, there's a fortune to be saved with a restaurant audit. You'll have to track the number of times they eat out, where they eat, and how much they spend for a whole month. Then you can show them how to cut the cost without cutting the fun. And you get a cut of the savings!

$-$$$$

The money you make will vary with how often your family eats out and how much they spend.

Kid's capital

This business will require very little time and no money at all.

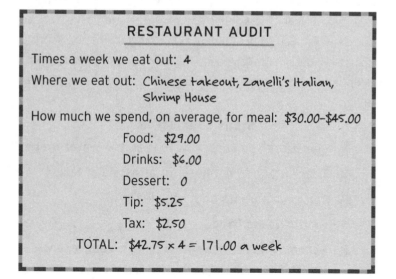

RESTAURANT AUDIT

Times a week we eat out: 4

Where we eat out: Chinese takeout, Zanelli's Italian, Shrimp House

How much we spend, on average, for meal: $30.00-$45.00

Food: $29.00

Drinks: $6.00

Dessert: 0

Tip: $5.25

Tax: $2.50

TOTAL: $42.75 × 4 = 171.00 a week

RESTAURANT REPORT

We can save $69.00 a week if we eat out one time a week instead of four.

Dinner with drinks at home = $20.00

$20.00 x 3 = $60.00

+ $42.00 for one family meal out

$102.00 instead of $171.00

TOTAL SAVINGS: $69.00

Skills

The skills needed are record keeping and human relations. You'll have to keep receipts and even menus to make the most effective money-saving plans. Food is a touchy subject; you'll have to make sure that your family is happy at meals and doesn't feel as though they are depriving themselves by not eating out as much.

Steps to success

Do the restaurant audit by filling in the form we've provided.

Cut costs by:

- $ **Using restaurant coupons** you find in mailers and local newspapers.

- $ **Ordering water** with lemon or lime, instead of soda.

- $ **Sharing large portions.** (Some restaurants will split dishes; others charge a little extra for the extra plate.)

- $ **Choosing from the children's menu** or asking for a child's portion if there is no separate menu.

$ **Setting a budget** before you even sit down to eat.

$ **Showing your parents** how much they could save by eating out less and cooking more.

$ **Taking a cut** of the savings.

As with the couponing business (Business 11, in chapter 19), joining wholesale clubs and looking for coupons will help lower your food costs and make money.

Business 19: Healthy Profits from Heat Audits

The big picture

Experts say that more heat is lost off the top of your head than from any other part of the body. So if you wear a hat, you keep 80 percent of the warmth in your body. A house is like that, too. If you do just a few things, you can save a big part of the fuel bill.

You don't have to know anything about heating or science to save lots of money in this business, but knowledge does help. You will learn a lot about energy as you go along. The best part is that your utility company will do an energy audit for you and teach you ways that you can save energy and money.

$$$$

If your family owns your house, this is probably the biggest money saver in the book.

Kid's capital

You don't need anything besides your time. But a few of your suggestions will take big money if your parents want to follow them.

Cutting waste on your heating bill will save your parents a lot of money. Also, you will feel more comfortable in the house.

Responsible Rhoda

Skills

You'll need lots of skills for this business, especially telephoning, organization (record keeping and filing), and human relations.

You will need to learn to read an electric meter. It has five numbered dials. The pointers on three of the dials turn clockwise, so read from left to right. The pointer always registers the number it has just passed. So if the pointer is between 3 and 4, read the number as 3. Next month read the dials again. That will tell you how many kilowatt-hours were used. (A kilowatt is a unit of energy.) Visit www.glps.net/meter-read.htm for more on reading electric meters.

Gas meters are read the same way, except there are four dials, two that move clockwise and two that move counter-clockwise. For more on gas meters, visit www.hydro.-mb.ca/your_service/how_to_read_meter_gas.shtml.

Use our sample heat audit in your home, and make sure your audit compares the costs with the savings.

HEAT AUDIT

1. **What kind of energy** heats your house: oil, gas, solar, or electric?

2. **What company** supplies the fuel (name, address, and telephone number)?

3. What was the **average monthly fuel bill** last year?

4. Do you have **storm windows?** These are extra windows that go over the regular windows in your house. They are expensive but can save fuel. Plastic sheets can, too, but they don't always look good.

5. Are there **air leaks?** Put your hand near doors and windows to find out.

6. If the house has an **oil burner,** when was the burner last cleaned? A cleaning needs to be done three times a year, and the filter should be changed every month.

7. Does **snow on your roof** melt fast? If your answer is yes, the insulation (the stuff between the walls and the outside of the house or roof) is not very good, and heat is leaking out.

8. Is there **insulation** around the water heater?

9. Do your **windows have drapes?** Drapes keep things warm but can also be expensive.

10. Do you have **attic fans?** They circulate heat in winter and draw cool air in summer.

11. Are any **windows broken?**

12. If you hold a **candle near a door or window**, does it blow out? Ask your parents for permission before you light a candle to do this test. If they say no, use a ribbon to see if it waves near a window or door.

How did your house do? Share your findings with your parents and other family members. If you found lots of problems, look at the suggestions we give later in this chapter, and try to help your parents make needed changes. Remember, the more money they save, the more you make!

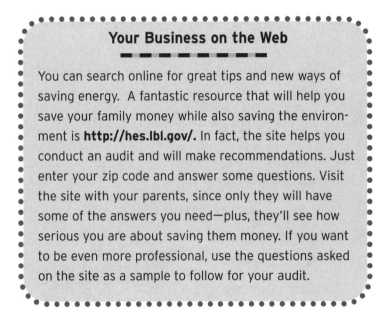

Your Business on the Web

You can search online for great tips and new ways of saving energy. A fantastic resource that will help you save your family money while also saving the environment is **http://hes.lbl.gov/.** In fact, the site helps you conduct an audit and will make recommendations. Just enter your zip code and answer some questions. Visit the site with your parents, since only they will have some of the answers you need—plus, they'll see how serious you are about saving them money. If you want to be even more professional, use the questions asked on the site as a sample to follow for your audit.

Steps to success

$ Study the **sample heat audit** we provided, and then do one of your home.

$ Ask the **energy conservation department** at your heating company to do a survey for you. Have your folks schedule it when they can be at home; never do it when you are alone.

§ Make your full **report to your family.** Be sure to include the costs of making changes.

§ Keep your family motivated with reports of **how much they save.**

§ **Get paid.**

Some things your family can do

Free:

§ Lower your thermostat in the winter; raise it in the summer.

§ Wear a sweater in the winter; wear shorts and T-shirts in the summer.

§ Close doors and windows.

For small amounts of money:

§ Clean the furnace and change the filters.

§ Use weather stripping.

§ Fix broken windows.

For a lot of money:

§ Put up drapes.

§ Install a new furnace.

§ Install an attic fan.

Not only do you save money on this job, but you help save the environment when you use less energy.

Candy Creditworthy

Business 20: Light Up Your Bank Account with Electricity Audits

The big picture

Like fuel and water, electricity is expensive. Also, you really can't see it, so it's easy to forget you are spending money every time a light or a TV is on.

Just by reading the electric meter, looking at the bill, and doing an audit, you can start saving money. Better yet, electric utility companies will do a survey for you and help you save.

$$$$

Most families really waste electricity, so savings can be big.

Kid's capital

This business is even better than heat- and water-waste management because the things you must do to save electricity are very inexpensive and mostly free. The capital you need is just your time.

Skills

The most important skill you will need is human relations. Turning on lights and other uses of electricity are habits.

You may meet with resistance when you first work with your family to save electricity. Use our sample electricity cost-management audit in your own home, and then share the results with your family.

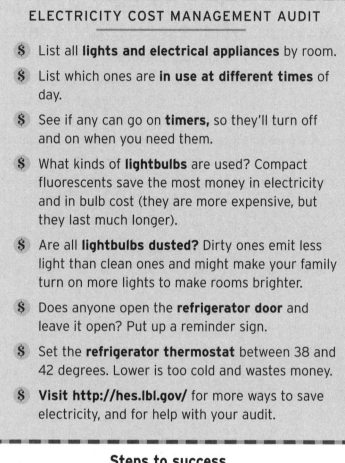

ELECTRICITY COST MANAGEMENT AUDIT

$ List all **lights and electrical appliances** by room.

$ List which ones are **in use at different times** of day.

$ See if any can go on **timers,** so they'll turn off and on when you need them.

$ What kinds of **lightbulbs** are used? Compact fluorescents save the most money in electricity and in bulb cost (they are more expensive, but they last much longer).

$ Are all **lightbulbs dusted?** Dirty ones emit less light than clean ones and might make your family turn on more lights to make rooms brighter.

$ Does anyone open the **refrigerator door** and leave it open? Put up a reminder sign.

$ Set the **refrigerator thermostat** between 38 and 42 degrees. Lower is too cold and wastes money.

$ **Visit http://hes.lbl.gov/** for more ways to save electricity, and for help with your audit.

Steps to success

$ Do the **electricity cost management audit.**

$ Arrange for your utility company to do an **electricity survey.** Be sure a parent or other adult is home; don't be home alone.

$ Write your **report.**

⑤ Call a family **waste management meeting.**

⑤ Keep track of the **utility bill.**

⑤ **Get paid!**

Ways to make extra money

Since this is a book about not wasting, we didn't want to waste any good ideas we had for making money. So here is a list of some other things you can do to save money and get a cut, although you probably wouldn't earn enough to build a separate business.

Laundry services

When we researched saving electricity, we found out that a clothes dryer costs almost fifty cents an hour to use. You can save the money and split the savings if you hang up the clothes instead of using the dryer. But doing that may not be worth the time. When compared with the time spent, the savings may not be enough for you—especially if you have lots of clothes.

But if you are good at ironing clothes, you can make money in a cost-efficient way with a home Laundromat. You can offer to wash your family's clothes in a washing machine, hang them in the basement or outside to dry, and then iron them. You probably have an iron in your house. If you don't, you can buy one for very little money. You might even get your parents to buy it; after all, it will save them money (don't worry, it won't add much to your electric bill). Of course, be careful while using an iron!

You could charge for the work, not just keep part of your family's savings. At first, this business may not sound good to you (especially if washing clothes seems like just a chore). However, owning a Laundromat can be a very good business. Some people who own real ones have whole chains of them and make a lot of money.

Disposables audit

Look for stuff your family throws out that all of you could save. For example, you can save aluminum foil to use twice, use cloth towels instead of paper towels, or flatten toilet paper rolls so they won't unravel as fast when you pull them.

Change scooping

Don't forget our deal with our dad (chapter 19). Ask if you can keep any change you find around the house.

Start a buying service

If your folks are planning to buy something big, like a refrigerator or car, offer to comparison shop for them. Go on the Web, look through newspapers, and call a number of places to get details. You can also use the classified ads to find what they want secondhand. Give them three leads, and let them follow up. Ask for payment for your time or for a percentage of their savings.

Junk art

If you are a good artist or craftsperson, you can turn junk into sculpture that you can sell at flea markets and garage sales.

The big Kahuna: Starting your own BIG business

What if you did all the jobs in the book? You would be a complete waste management consultant. Wow! It's possible. Just start with the one that fits you best. Get that business going. Once it's in place, start another business just like it, but in a different area. This is called business expansion. Soon your business might look like this:

BIG KAHUNA, INC.

Waste Management Specialist

Utility management ←

Water management ←

Clothes management ←

Food management ←

You can expand in a lot of ways. You can keep your waste management business and also go into the resale clothes business we told you about in chapter 14. If you ran all these unrelated businesses, you would be a conglomerate. Some famous *conglomerates* are Vivendi and General Electric.

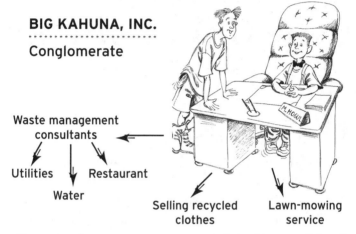

BIG KAHUNA, INC.
Conglomerate

Waste management consultants

Utilities   Restaurant

Water

Selling recycled clothes

Lawn-mowing service

You can take on new customers and do the same thing for your neighbors as you do for your family. This approach is a *lateral expansion*.

BIG KAHUNA, INC.
Waste Management Specialist
Customer list

Strangers who become clients   Relatives   Parents   Neighbors

Coca-Cola is one company that has used lateral expansion. They buy companies that make different kinds of beverages, and then Coca-Cola sells all those—along with Coke—in the United States, China, Russia, and other countries.

You can make the supplies you need instead of buying them and even sell those supplies. This practice is called a *vertical expansion.*

BIG KAHUNA, INC.

Lemonade Company

Grow lemons   Sell lemonade   Sell lemons to other retailers of lemonade

Companies expand vertically by buying companies that make the supplies they need, so they no longer have to buy the supplies themselves.

No matter how you decide to grow your business, you should always think about how to make it more profitable and useful to your community. Those two things often go hand-in-hand. Always remember it's your business, which means the sky is the limit. Your imagination and energy can make *your* business dreams a reality.

Epilogue:

Ten fun activities that make parents and kids business-brilliant

(a final note from Mom to Parents)

by Adriane G. Berg

Business acumen is not a matter of luck, inheritance, or even formal education. It is a matter of doing certain things right all the time. After thirty years of studying impressive business successes, I know what those things are. They are simple, commonsense things—the things that keep you shopping at certain stores, visiting the same dentist, and buying at the same flower shop no matter what the competition does. In my own business, the more I do these things, the more I prosper, and vice versa.

Here are my top-ten business habits and how to teach them to—or learn them with—your kids. You can have fun with these even if your child is not engaged in business at the moment. Just raising consciousness about these business bonanzas is a great step in the right direction.

Be liked and respected

1. Thank someone: Who gave you a helping hand recently? Did anyone do a job that was top-notch? It could be the local pizza delivery person who brought the pizza while it was still hot. It could be a camp counselor or someone you asked for advice on saving energy. If you try, you and your child can think of lots of people to thank. Make a list and then thank them in writing. If you know who their boss is, send that person a duplicate of your thank-you note.

This exercise can be fun, and it helps you make and keep friends. But why does it help with business success? Help your child write down all the ways. Here are some ideas:

- § It wins you **new customers.**
- § It leads to **referrals.**
- § It gets you better **personal and business service.**
- § The people you thank **remember you.**
- § **You stand out** from the world of grouches and killjoys everyone meets each day.

The business world spends a fortune on fruit baskets and other corporate gifts as thank-yous. In fact, such purchases add up to a million-dollar industry in itself. But one personal note is worth much more than a calendar or a pen with your company's name on it.

Watch newspapers, television, and magazines for all the ways businesses try to be nice, such as coupons, giveaways, prizes, sales, and promises. Discuss which ones you and your child find effective.

2. Do something nice for someone: How many opportunities did you and your child have to do a good turn today? Write them down. Did you do them? Why? Why not? The philanthropist Milton Gralla, who built a megabusiness starting with twenty thousand dollars, says, "Nice guys finish first." After publishing trade journals in every industry, he confirms that the folks at the top constantly do good deeds.

Is a friend out of school because of illness? Get homework assignments to him without being asked. Could your grandma use a loving phone call? Make it. Is it your mailman's birthday? Send a card.

Note

Activities 1 and 2 can be done independently of any business your child is in. They are wonderful social habits that naturally enhance business skills in later years. But if your child does have a hobby, business, sport, or other focus, do the activities in that context. For example, when Arthur tried couponing, he found certain checkout people fast and pleasant, and he decided they were good candidates for thank-yous. He also found coupons that we couldn't use but that our neighbors with pets could. To him, they were good candidates for a good deed.

Did we get any paybacks for our thoughtfulness? In fact, we did. But that's not the point. It's the deed itself that does the trick. Still, when Arthur entered one of the regular supermarkets and saw the sign reading "Cash Register Closed" magically vanish, he knew his shopping time would be shorter!

Know how your business is doing

3. Keep records: This book contains examples of many different types of records, from invoices to contracts. A great experiment is to study something every day for a month, with and without record keeping. You and your child will be amazed at the difference in your control and knowledge of the subject when you rely only on memory, as compared with documentation.

For example, make a survey of your family's television-watching habits. Who watches what? When do they watch? How do they feel about the program? Try that for one month and then share a report with the whole family.

Repeat the survey with a form you create, a time chart, and a viewer-satisfaction questionnaire. At the end of the second month, see how much more you know, how concrete your results are, and how you can use the information to change bad habits, cut down on viewing, increase quality choices, and so on.

4. Write down your business purpose and major profit center—then focus on those: Especially if you are a hard and dedicated worker, it's easy to forget why you are working. If your child has a business, review with him or her what the business's purpose is and where the most money is made—that is, identify the major profit center. Encourage your child to connect efforts with results. For example, if most business comes from one neighborhood, your child can increase efforts in that neighborhood.

If your child is not immediately involved with a business, check out neighborhood businesses. Entrepreneurs love to talk to you. Local bankers, restaurant owners, and dry cleaners will let you know how they see their profit center, where they have made their mistakes, and how they learned to concentrate their efforts most effectively.

Innovate

5. Think of one new way people can hear of your business—then implement it: Balloons, T-shirts, flyers, sky writing—ways to get known are endless. Experiment with your own business. If you don't have a business, keep a list of all the marketing techniques you and your child noticed throughout the week, from sidewalk sales to radio ads. I bet you will come up with at least one new idea in a week's time.

6. Think of one new way you can make money— then implement it: It takes creativity to make money. But an object in motion tends to stay in motion, and a good business tends to expand. If you use a product in your business, can you also manufacture it and sell it to others? Is there a related service you could perform? Why not water the plants while you are baby-sitting?

Look at chapter 21 to see how you can help your child become a conglomerate.

Be cost-effective

7. Determine one useless or inefficient thing you are doing—then eliminate it: Parents may have a longer list than kids would. The list can include business, personal, or social wheel spinning. This exercise often also requires a change in habits. Report to each other on your progress, and share the problems you experience while changing your ways.

8. Institute at least one time-saving device: Do the same as what you did in item 7, but concentrate on something that will save you time—learning a new computer skill, using a barber closer to your home or workplace, or buying in bulk. Time-saving steps and devices sometimes cost money in the beginning, but they are worth it.

Compete

9. Check the competition: If your child is in a business with visible competition, help him or her list the things needed for comparisons: pricing, quality, hours of operation, advertising, and marketing. If there are no competing businesses, pick two car dealers, banks, or hair salons in your community and compare them. Which is doing better? Why?

10. Play pricing games. To lower prices, you must buy raw material cheaper, make less of a profit on each item, or lower the quality. Can any of these steps be done? Is making the change worth it? Will taking this step result in higher volume or in lower volume, because of a decrease in quality? Are you better off with higher prices for more service, better quality, or faster service? How are competitors pricing their products or services?

Books to read

Alexander, Sue. *Finding Your First Job*. New York: Dutton, 1980.

Armstrong, Louise. *How to Turn Up into Down into Up: A Child's Guide to Inflation, Depression, and Economic Recovery*. New York: Harcourt Brace Jovanovich, 1976.

Berg, Adriane G. *Your Wealth-Building Years: Financial Planning for 18-to 38-Year-O1ds*. 3rd ed. New York: Newmarket Press, 1995.

Drew, Bonnie. *Moneyskills*. Hawthorne, N.J.: Career Press, 1992.

Drew, Bonnie, and Noel Drew. *Fast Cash for Kids*. Hawthorne, N.J.: Career Press, 1991.

BOOKS TO READ

————. *Kid Biz*. Austin, Tex.: Eakin Press, 1990.

Ellison, Cheri, and Debbie Hope. *Kids Bias Game Plan*. Dana Point, Calif.: ExecuSystems, 1993. A complete system for teaching kids business responsibility in the home without outside jobs; includes contracts, parenting guide, and more. Call 1-800-735-3378.

Gelb, Eric. *Checkbook Management—A Guide to Saving Money*. Woodmere, N.Y.: Career Advancement Center, Inc., 1994.

Henry, Joanne L. *Bernard Baruch*. New York: Bobbs-Merrill, 1991.

Hoban, Lillian. *Arthur's Funny Money*. New York: Harper & Row, 1981.

Kanarek, Lisa. *101 Home Office Success Secrets*. Hawthorne, N.J.: Career Press, 1993.

Laeberman, Marc R. *Your Rights as a Consumer*. Hawthorne, N.J.: Career Press, 1994.

Lesko, Matthew. *The Great American Gripe Book*. Kensington, Md.: Information USA, 1991.

Levy, Richard C., and Ronald O. Weingartner. *From Workshop to Toy Store*. New York: Simon & Schuster, 1992.

McQuown, Judith H. *Use Your Own Corporation to Get Rich*. New York: Simon & Schuster, 1991.

BOOKS TO READ

New Workbook for Women. Andover, Mass.: 1982, 1988.

Outten, Wayne N., with Noah A. Kinigstein. *The Rights of Employees.* New York: Bantam Books, 1984.

Parinello, Al. *On the Air.* Hawthorne, N.J.: Career Press, 1990.

Phillips, Carole. *The New Money Workbook for Women.* Amherst, N.H.: Brick House Publishing, 1988.

Publicity Outlets. New Milford, Conn.: Harold Hansen Publishers, 1995.

Shanaman, Fred. *The First Official Money Making Book for Kids.* New York: Bantam Books, 1983.

Von Hoelscher, Russ. *How You Can Make a Fortune Selling Information by Mail.* San Diego, Calif.: Profit Ideas, 1987.

Wallace, David. *How to Turn Lemons into Money: Money Basics.* Englewood Cliffs, N.J.: Prentice-Hall, 1984.

Weinstein, Grace W. *Children and Money.* New York: New American Library, 1985.

Weiss, Elizabeth H. *More Free Stuff for Kids.* Deephaven, Minn..: Meadowbrook Press, 1993.

Wendover, Robert W. *Two-Minute Motivation.* Naperville, Ill.: Sourcebooks, 1995.

Zeitz, Baila, and Lorraine Dusky. *The Best Companies for Women.* New York: Simon & Schuster, 1988.

Index

INDEX

INDEX

INDEX

About the Authors

Arthur Bochner wrote *The Totally Awesome Money Book for Kids* with his mother when he was eleven years old and *The Totally Awesome Business Book for Kids* when he was thirteen. Now twenty-five, he's a political speechwriter in Washington, D.C.

Rose Bochner, Arthur's fifteen-year-old sister, was nominated for the Distinguished Students Award at her New Jersey middle school. She's a rock climber and plans to teach.

Adriane G. Berg is a renowned speaker, attorney, and leader in the field of finance and aging. She is the author of a dozen books on personal finance, the wife of Stuart Bochner, and the mother of Arthur and Rose.

Stuart Bochner is President of the Foundation for Free Enterprise, a New Jersey–based not-for-profit organization that presents educational programs to high schools and middle schools in the areas of free enterprise, economics, finances, and entrepreneurship.

More Newmarket Press Books for Young Readers

Totally Awesome Books by Arthur Bochner and Rose Bochner

The New Totally Awesome Money Book for Kids
Named by the *American Library Association* as a "Best Book of the Year," this popular guide for 8- to 14-year-olds includes quizzes, games, forms, charts, stories, and drawings on the basics of saving, investing, borrowing, working, and taxes. 192 pages. Drawings. Glossary. Index. 5 $\frac{3}{16}$" x 8". 978-1-55704-738-0. $9.95. Paperback.

The New Totally Awesome Business Book for Kids
This fun, fact-filled guide for 8- to 14-year-olds includes quizzes, games, cartoons, and all the information a young person needs to know about starting up a business. 192 pages. Drawings. Glossary. Index. 5 $\frac{3}{16}$" x 8". 978-1-55704-757-1. $9.95. Paperback.

The Junior Su Doku Series
Created especially for kids ages 8 and up, each edition boasts over 110 puzzles that involve numbers, words, and shapes, ranging from easy 4 x 4 grids to the more challenging 6 x 6 and classic 9 x 9 puzzles.

Junior Su Doku
112 pages. 122 puzzles. 5 $\frac{3}{16}$" x 8 $\frac{1}{4}$". 978-1-55704-706-9. $4.95. Paperback.

Junior Su Doku Valentine's Day
With Valentine's Day–themed words and shapes!
128 pages. 136 puzzles. 5 $\frac{3}{16}$" x 8 $\frac{1}{4}$". 978-1-55704-713-7. $4.95. Paperback.

Junior Su Doku Easter
With Easter-themed words and shapes!
128 pages. 136 puzzles. 5 $\frac{3}{16}$" x 8 $\frac{1}{4}$". 978-1-55704-715-1. $4.95. Paperback.

Junior Su Doku Halloween
With Halloween–themed words and shapes!
128 pages. 130 puzzles. 5 $\frac{3}{16}$" x 8 $\frac{1}{4}$". 978-1-55704-730-4. $4.95. Paperback.

Junior Su Doku Christmas
With Christmas–themed words and shapes!
128 pages. 111 puzzles. 5 $\frac{3}{16}$" x 8 $\frac{1}{4}$". 978-1-55704-707-6. $4.95. Paperback.

Kidoku
The ultimate puzzle book for kids, featuring five different kinds of puzzles and logic games including Su Doku.
224 pages. 204 puzzles. 5 $\frac{3}{16}$" x 8 $\frac{1}{4}$". 978-1-55704-720-5. $6.95. Paperback.

FICTION FOR YOUNG READERS

Akeelah and the Bee
A Novel by James W. Ellison
Based on the screenplay by Doug Atchison
An inspirational drama about Akeelah Anderson, a precocious 11-year-old girl from South Los Angeles with a gift for words.
192 pages. 5 ¼" x 8". 978-1-55704-729-8. $6.95. Paperback.

Finding Forrester
A Novel by James W. Ellison
Based on the screenplay by Mike Rich
The inspiring story of the unlikely friendship between a famous, reclusive novelist and an amazingly gifted teen who secretly yearns to be a writer.
192 pages. 5 ¼" x 8". 978-1-55704-479-2. $9.95. Paperback.

Fly Away Home
A Novel by Patricia Hermes
Based on the Screenplay Written by Robert Rodat and Vince McKewin
Adapted from the film by the award-winning author of *Kevin Corbett Eats Flies* and *My Girl*, this inspirational family adventure follows 14-year-old Amy and her inventor father as they attempt to teach geese how to fly.
160 pages. 5 ³⁄₁₆" x 7 ⅞". 978-1-55704-489-1. $7.95. Paperback.

Two Brothers: The Tales of Kumal and Sangha
A Novel by James W. Ellison
Based on the Screenplay by Alain Godard & Jean-Jacques Annaud
Inspired by the acclaimed family film from the maker of *The Bear*, a heartwarming nature tale about two tiger cubs born in the Southeast Asian jungle.
192 pages. 5 ³⁄₁₆" x 7 ⅞". 978-1-55704-632-1. $7.95. Paperback.

THREE CLASSIC WILDERNESS TALES BY JAMES OLIVER CURWOOD

The Bear
Thor, a mighty grizzly, and Muskwa, a motherless bear cub, become companions in the Canadian wilderness in this exciting story that inspired the film *The Bear.*
208 pages. 5 ³⁄₁₆" x 7 ⅞". 978-1-55704-131-9. $5.95. Paperback.

Baree, The Story of a Wolf-Dog
The thrilling "timeless tale" (*ALA Booklist*) of a half-tame, half-wild wolf pup who must survive alone in the Canadian wilderness.
256 pages. 5 ³⁄₁₆" x 7 ⅞". 978-1-55704-132-6. $5.95. Paperback.

Kazan, Father of Baree
The truly unforgettable story of Kazan, the mightiest canine of the Canadian wilderness.
240 pages. 5 ³⁄₁₆" x 7 ⅞". 978-1-55704-225-5. $5.95. Paperback.

THE "WHAT'S HAPPENING TO MY BODY?" SERIES
THE BESTSELLING GUIDES FOR PRETEENS AND TEENS
BY LYNDA MADARAS AND AREA MADARAS

The "What's Happening to My Body?" Book for Girls
This classic book covers the body's changing size and shape, breasts, the reproductive organs, the menstrual cycle, pubic hair, puberty in boys, diet, exercise, health, and much more.
288 pages. Drawings. Index. 6 ⅛" x 9 ¼".
978-1-55704-764-9. $12.95. Paperback • 978-1-55704-768-7. $24.95. Hardcover.

The "What's Happening to My Body?" Book fo[r]
The classic puberty education book for boys covers
and shape, hair, voice changes, perspiration, pimple[s]
sexuality, puberty in girls, and much more.
256 pages. Drawings. Index. 6 ⅛" x 9 ¼".
978-1-55704-765-6. $12.95. Paperback • 978-1-55704-769-4

My Body, My Self for Girls
Fun and fact-filled—over 100 quizzes, checklists, ga[mes]
your changing body.
160 pages. Illustrations. 6 ⅛" x 9 ¼". 978-1-55704-766-3. $1[2]

My Body, My Self for Boys
Fun and fact-filled—over 100 quizzes, checklists, ga[mes]
your changing body.
128 pages. Illustrations. 6 ⅛" x 9 ¼". 978-1-55704-767-0. $1[2]

Ready, Set, Grow!
A "What's Happening to My Body?" Book for [Y]
Written especially for 8–11-year-old girls and playfu[l]
toon drawings, Ready, Set, Grow! covers all the ne[w]
can expect.
128 pages. Illustrations. Index. 7" x 7".
978-1-55704-565-2. $12.00. Paperback • 978-1-55704-587-4

For postage and handling, please add $5.00 for the first book, plus
and availability are subject to change. Please call 800-669-3903 to
I enclose a check or money order payable to **Newmarket Press** in

Name _____

Address _____

City/State/Zip _____

E-mail Address _____

For discounts on orders of five or more copies or to get a catalog, contact Newmarket Press
Sales Department, 18 East 48th Street, New York, NY 10017; phone 212-832-3575 or
800-669-3903; fax 212-832-3629; or e-mail sales@newmarketpress.com
www.newmarketpress.com